, care ?

Gerald O'Mahony S.J.

THE TWO-EDGED GOSPEL

For Eileen, Richard and Anita

THE TWO-EDGED GOSPEL

GIFT AND INVITATION

Gerald O'Mahony, SJ

GRACEWING

First published in 1995 by Eagle

This edition published in 2005
by
Gracewing Publishing
2 Southern Avenue, Leominster
Herefordshire HR6 0QF

The right of Gerald O'Mahony to be identified as author of this work has been asserted in accordance with the Copyright, Designs and patents Act 1988.

ISBN 0 85244 638 1

Printed in England

CONTENTS

CHAPTER 1

THE TWO-EDGED GOSPEL

The gospel of Jesus Christ is two-edged. We know from the Letter to the Hebrews that 'the word of God is ... sharper than any two-edged sword' (Hebrews 4:12), and there are, I believe, two edges to the Good News throughout the New Testament; this is what I wish to investigate. The reason why I think it important is that if the sword cuts in the wrong direction first, it damages the one holding the sword, instead of the enemy.

The gospel is a word, a good word, good tidings. The speaker is God, the listener is any human being. The first thing is to listen. Then, when we have listened, comes the invitation from God to say something back. So I say something back, and the word has become active in me: there is a conversation. Perhaps that illustrates clearly the importance of getting the two things, listening and speaking, in the right order. In my capacity as creature, it is polite and indeed necessary to listen *first*, and only then to make a reply suitable to what has been spoken to me.

When God speaks to us human beings, he uses what is for us a new language, and we cannot presume to have understood it right away. The disciples of Jesus clearly took a long, wearisome time to realize what Jesus was really saying to them. Even today, when we have the whole gospel story before us from the start, we find we are always learning. Particularly, we are inclined to make our replies to God before we have properly understood, and then inevitably we find this difficult. The cross of Jesus is painful and a madness if we have not first understood the terms on which we are invited to take up the cross. Once God's terms are understood, the sting goes out of the pain, even though there still is pain in life.

There is the same two-sidedness in the sacramental life of the Church. The sacraments can feel like a burden or a blessing, depending on how one holds the sword. The same goes for the spiritual life of Christians and their prayer: there can be a spirit of competition and exclusiveness even in prayer and the search for holiness, or else prayer and the spiritual life can be completely free from competition and an easy yoke.

There is in all of us a tendency to expect what is free to be costly, and what is costly to be free, when it comes to our faith. Conversion is free, salvation is free. All we have to do for conversion is to turn round and find love never left us. For some obscure reason we seem always to want to pay for our forgiveness, instead of saving our currency for what really is costly.

Listening is free; it is the reply that is costly. God speaks to us in the language of love, and to be loved costs nothing. But to love in return is costly, and in our perversity we would rather that loving in return was free. Such is God's courtesy that the only thing he demands of us costs nothing. The difficult, the costly things, are all voluntary. I shall be saying these things over and over again in the course of this book, but I do hope to show by the repetition that the two-sidedness of the gospel is very much there in the evidence, and not a figment of my imagination.

Here to begin with is a list which will grow longer as this investigation continues. The images all appear in the Gospels, those in the left-hand column are to do with listening to God, whereas those on the right have to do with the response. We will be seeing that Jesus tells the same message over and over again, using different images. So, for example, we find in the Gospels:

lamb	shepherd
enlightened	light for others
little child	power
son/daughter	servant
built on rock	rock for others
fish	fisher
coin	coin seeker
sown with seed	sower (fruitful)
guided on the way	guide

Let me start with the lamb and the shepherd.

CHAPTER 2

THE LAMB
AND THE SHEPHERD

There are three strange things about the lamb in the New Testament: first, that God should be bothered with it; second, that the lamb should become a shepherd; third, that the lamb should become a shepherd without ceasing to be a lamb.

The Christian life is like a symphony in four movements. First, God loves me, his creature, with no limits and no conditions, and for no reason. After that, it is up to me to listen to God's love and believe in it: that makes the second movement of the symphony. The third movement is an invitation, from God to me, to show my gratitude to God by loving my fellow-creatures. The fourth movement is my attempt to respond to the invitation by a generous life.

The story of the lamb and the shepherd easily becomes an example of the movements of the symphony. Lambs and sheep once domesticated are pretty helpless creatures. Jesus had pity on the crowds who followed him because, he said, they were like sheep without a shepherd. He told a parable about a sheep that got lost, and how the shepherd left the ninety-nine orderly sheep and went in search of the stray. When he found it, he did not beat it or shout at it, he did not even make it walk home: he picked it up and carried it home on his shoulders, rejoicing and calling on his friends to rejoice with him. As in all Jesus' parables I, the reader or listener, am invited to identify with the central character of the story, namely in this case the lost sheep or lamb. As such, Jesus

is saying that I belong to him as the Shepherd from before
ever the story began, and that no matter what I do he will
still cherish me. If I should manage to stay safely with the
ninety-nine, all is well; if I should stray from the fold, he
will come and fetch me, so all is well. Jesus is stating the
first movement of the symphony, and he is leaving it up
to me to make the jump of faith in his love that creates
the second movement.

In the third movement the initiative is once again
God's. There is no way a lamb can become a shepherd in
ordinary life. Lambs and sheep do not become shepherds.
Yet Jesus clearly invites those who would be his disciples
to become shepherds once they have learnt thoroughly
how to become lambs. Once we have experienced being
forgiven in spite of the perverse way we went astray,
then we begin to know what shepherding is all about,
and we can begin to be trusted as assistant shepherds
to Jesus. Peter the apostle is a clear example: he thought
he knew all about being a shepherd and a leader, until he
denied Jesus and learnt his own desperate weakness. In
the event it was only then, after going badly astray and
being forgiven so easily afterwards, that he truly became
a lamb and fit to become the shepherd Jesus had called
him to be.

There are, therefore, two clear halves to the symphony.
The first half has to do with being a lamb of God. The
second has to do with being a shepherd. These are the
two edges of the gospel, and if we neglect the first and
try to go straight onto the second, we will end up being
wounded.

The original Shepherd is God, the one Jesus called
his Father. Already in the Old Testament the image
is well established. Abraham must have found that his
own relationship with God reminded him of the way he
looked after his sheep and lambs as a nomadic family
man. King David seems to have started life as a shepherd
boy working for his father. The prophet Ezekiel tells how
God will come himself (or is it his servant David?) to
take the sheep away from the under-shepherds who

were neglecting or exploiting them, to feed them and care for them properly himself. Time and again the prophets and other writers use the image of sheep with their shepherd.

Jesus comes as the Lamb of God, chosen, precious, eventually to lead but first to demonstrate what it is to be a lamb before God. In the Gospel of John, Jesus is Lamb of God at the start, Shepherd at the finish, laying down his life for his sheep. In the other Gospels, Jesus listens first, while the voice from heaven calls him beloved. Only then does he begin to select his under-shepherds, his disciples, and only then to start taking the crowds away from the shepherds they already had, to feed them himself on the green grass by the clear waters. Even Jesus is Lamb first, Shepherd second, without ceasing to be Lamb. Unlike Peter, he gets the order of priority right first time.

Jesus insists that each of us become one of his sheep or lambs; as for being shepherds, yes, he invites his sheep and lambs to become shepherds, but he does not insist. To be a lamb is compulsory; to be a shepherd is voluntary. In order to be saved by Jesus, I need no other qualifications than to be a lost lamb, bleating loudly. Jesus works as the Chief Shepherd in a world where there are many wolves and where there is much confusion in the flock. As Christians we are invited, once we know well our status as lambs, to help in the shepherding. But God is the owner of the sheep, Jesus is the Chief Shepherd, and if my contribution is not very successful, the responsibility for eventual success is not mine. I am more in the nature of a sheepdog, in British culture, than a fully responsible shepherd. If I let sheep escape, the Chief Shepherd will cover for me.

There is a famous prayer of St Teresa of Avila in which she says that Christ has no body now but ours, no hands but ours, no feet but ours to do his work with and go where he wants. Yes and no. Yes he wishes to work through our hands, our feet, our hearts; but no, he does not actually need my heart to get through to someone else's heart. He deigns to use me, but he is not limited to or by me. He has other and more direct ways into another's heart if need be.

In this symphony I have been speaking about, there seem to be two movements depending on God – he loves me and he invites me – and two movements that seem to depend rather on me: to listen and to respond. How do I set about listening? How does the lost lamb stuck in the brambles recognize the voice of the Shepherd and tell it apart from the voice of a wolf? Only by the peace, and the relief. So little is asked for by my Shepherd, only that I let myself be rescued. To let myself be loved, to let myself be called 'beloved' by the Truth, even though I only see myself as hateful. To let myself be precious to my Shepherd, even though I ran away. To let myself be loved simply for being his, not for being a successful sheep or lamb.

Such, then, is the shape of the gospel under the image of lamb and shepherd. Without always going into such detail regarding other gospel images, I would like to show just how many there are besides, that follow the same twofold pattern. Usually, too, on each side there will be a dialogue: God loves; I trust. God invites; I come. One symphony, two halves, four movements.

CHAPTER 3

ENLIGHTENED LIGHT

At first sight, it would seem as strange for darkness to become light as for a lamb to become a shepherd. But then we think of mirrors, and other kinds of reflection. Moonlight has a special quality, simply by being a dark mass that the sun shines on. Our own earth is revealed as dark once the sun goes down.

The shepherd claims the lamb as his own; the light shines on a dark object and enlightens it. One of the early titles for baptism was 'enlightenment'. The light of God's unquestioning love shines on the human creature, and the creature becomes full of light. But in a relationship such as this, the one being loved has to face the light. Just as the lamb had to bleat and then let itself be rescued and picked up, the person in the dark has to turn round and face the light of God's love and forgiveness.

Ultimately there is only one source of the light which is love, namely God. If we have been running away from God, all we can ever see is darkness, since the light is behind us and there is no other light. All we can see is shadow, and our own shadow mocks us. But no matter how far or how fast we have run, all we ever have to do to set things right between us and God is to turn round. Conversion means turning round. We tend to think we must have a lot of ground to make up before we can be at rights with God again, but no ... there are no distances with God. To see God's love is for all to be well. These then are the first two movements of the symphony interpreted in light: first, God's light is always shining; second, the human creature turns round to face the light. After living with shadows, the human realizes that he or she is nothing but a mirror, not the source of light but only a being capable of receiving and reflecting the light.

The surfaces upon which we receive the light are our eyes, our ears and in a certain sense our tongues. Facing God we see that he loves us with an everlasting love; listening to God we hear his voice telling of his love for us; with our tongues we tell him we have seen and heard the message. In the second movement of the symphony, therefore, we look at what God does and has done; we listen, and we then assure God that we have heard.

In the other, costly, phase of the gospel, which I am calling the third and fourth movements of the symphony, God first of all invites the mirror which I am to turn and shine the light I have received upon others, especially upon those who are still in the dark. To put it in a slightly different way, I remember that in my baptism there was a candle lit for me from the paschal candle, and that little light was all for me. If I had been big enough I would have done what I can now do in imagination, namely held the candle close to my heart as a symbol of God's personal love for me. But then at some later stage in my life, always later, God invites me to hold up my candle so that others in the house can see what they are about. Then I become conscious that I am going to be colder myself and less aware of the light as a personal gift. Such is the third movement of the symphony, interpreted in light. The fourth movement comes when I hold up my candle, and discover that I can actually see more, not less . . . and the light is still safe in my own hand to bring to my heart when I have need of it.

The light I am invited to reflect is obviously the same light I received in the first place. I am to invite others to see that God's light and love is still shining no less brightly when my back is turned; that I am still God's beloved lamb when I stray, and that he never ceases to call me his beloved. And just as the lamb became a shepherd without ceasing to be a lamb, so the new little light becomes a light for others without ceasing to be no-light in itself.

We receive our light from Jesus, but even Jesus is 'light from light', and not himself the source of the light. He too is a mirror, the mirror-image of the unseen God. He does not speak simply from himself, but he speaks only what his Father gives him to speak. He speaks unquestioning love. God is Light; then Jesus states publicly more than once, 'I am the light of the world'; lastly he says to his disciples, 'You are the light of the world' (Matthew 5:14). He does not say this to the world at large, only to his disciples who have heard his call and voluntarily joined him as mirrors of the light.

Little Child and Power

The same realities in other images are expressed by the separation of 'little child' and 'power'. To begin with I believe I am an adult and in charge of my own destiny. To enter into the world of the gospel I have to come to the realization that I am weak and I am mortal, but God is saying my weakness does not matter if I will only let him take care of it. Saint Thérèse of Lisieux who was a powerful young woman by human standards, compared herself to an infant learning to crawl who tries to climb the stairs to reach her father at the top. She keeps tumbling down as many steps as she conquers, until in the end her father comes down, picks her up and carries her upstairs.

How does the weakness of the little child turn into power without ceasing to be the weakness of a little child? Many a time I have seen little children crossing a busy road in the safety and strength of an adult, their mother perhaps, or as we have had in Britain for many years now, a 'Lollipop lady' with a lollipop-shaped pole to hold up and stop the traffic. One little child holds the free hand of the adult, and another little child holds the other hand of the first child. Thus the strength and the wisdom of the adult is passing through one child to the next. The in-between child remains a child and weak, but is able to guide the other in the strength of the adult.

Thus in Christianity I know that I am unable to save myself or to find forgiveness unless God freely gives it through Jesus, a fact which makes me constantly rely on God and not on myself. On those terms I can assist others who come to me to find the way through dangers, so long as I remain conscious all the time of my own nothingness. If I let go of God's hand and try to do the guiding all by myself, I am in as much danger as one little child leading another across a busy main road.

The four movements of the symphony interpreted in weakness and power are, first, power is there in God for me; second, I let myself be forgiven, led, or picked up and carried; third, I am invited to take hold of other weak people without losing hold of God; fourth, I do as invited. I call these four movements 'movements' and not 'stages' because the whole process is like a symphony that can be, and is, played over and over again, but always in that order. We can never say we have done with the previous movement, because it will come round again.

In Jesus is weakness and power: both edges of the gospel are present first in him. He had infinitely more than we have of which to empty himself and to become a little child in a literal sense. But his emptying of himself went much further than that, as we shall be reminded when it comes to his being called the Servant. His weakness shows best in his unwillingness ever to do what was simply his own will. He was listening all the time, staying in the light, waiting for the right time before 'crossing the dangerous road'. And because he waited and found himself at the right time, he was and is able to take other little children by the hand and guide them across.

Because he did things in the right order, not going his own way unassisted, he received power from the One who was leading him and carrying him. He was transfigured,

he will be seen as the Son of man coming on the clouds
of heaven with great power, his very cross became a
glory, and he had the power to send the Spirit once
God had raised him from the dead and he had ascended
to glory.

CHAPTER 4

WHICH WAY UP?

There is a right way and a wrong way of holding a sword. In the case of the two-edged sword which is the gospel, the wrong way to hold it is the Old Testament way. Jesus had warnings about not trying to put new wine in old wineskins, and not to patch an old garment with new cloth. To wield the gospel in an Old Testament way results in the holder being cut instead of cutting.

Jesus turned Old Testament morality upside down. There is in the Old Testament a fairly constant theme stating that if, and only if, the people obey God's commands, then, and only then, will God be faithful to them. Without anything like an exhaustive search, I have found such statements in Exodus, in Leviticus, twice in Deuteronomy, in Joshua, in the First Book of Kings, and even in such a late book as Ecclesiasticus. Psalm 119 is an enormous song in praise of the privilege of knowing exactly what God wants, so as to be sure of God's love in return. Not surprisingly, the 176th and final verse of the psalm is a cry for help to the Shepherd by the lost sheep, who could not keep up with all the commands, decrees, ordinances, statutes, precepts, laws and testimonies, but has gone astray.

As the centuries went by, what seems to have happened is that it dawned on some of the prophets that the old way of looking at the relationship with God was less wonderful than the whole truth. The Old Covenant as expressed by Moses was designed along the lines of a covenant between the ruler of an empire and the last and least of his subject peoples: 'The empire has the

power. If you join our alliance and keep all the laws
and decrees of the empire, then the Emperor will protect
you. If you disobey the rules seriously, you are in danger
of being cut off from the empire and destroyed rather
than protected.' The mystery that began to dawn on the
prophets was that God was infinitely more forgiving than
any earthly emperor would ever be. No matter how many
times the people disobeyed, they still found God willing to
pick up the pieces and start again. Somehow the covenant
was starting to look everlasting, so how should the New
Covenant be expressed, and who would be the one to
formulate it?

The Old Covenant, then, started on the ground, and
aimed at heaven. Having reached heaven, it would then
travel back to earth with God's love and protection. A
suitable diagram for it, therefore, would be two doorposts
and a lintel: up from the ground, across, then down again
to earth. The New Covenant of Jesus is the other way
up. His covenant starts from above, from God, with the
totally unquestioning love that only God can claim as
rightful property. It comes down to earth, to us, with
God's guaranteed love, no matter what we do. If we
accept it for what it is, God then invites our love in return
to travel upwards to heaven. The doorposts have been
turned upside down, and now make a letter 'U' shape.
God loves; I trust. God calls; I come. The central model
Jesus gave was the relationship between a child and the
one the child calls 'Abba', the intimate word for Father.
Clearly from the context of Jesus' teaching, especially in
the parables, the force behind it is that 'Abba' loves the
children not because they are good children, but because
they are children of 'Abba'. 'I love you, not because you
are good but because you are mine.'

Two clear examples may be chosen from the many
in the New Testament to illustrate the change that
Jesus brought about. First, the story of Zacchaeus (Luke
19:1–10). Jesus did not say to Zacchaeus up in the tree,
'If, and only if, you will keep all God's laws, ordinances,
precepts and decrees, I shall come and take a meal with

you'. Much more than that, Jesus did not say, 'If you give
half your money to the poor, and if you agree to pay back
fourfold for any defrauding you have done, then I will
come to your place for supper'. No, Jesus reflecting his
Father's love put no conditions. Simply, in friendship, he
gave Zacchaeus acceptance. The surprise and delight this
approach gave to the tax collector was such that he not
only promised to be law-abiding, but he went far beyond
the letter of the law in his generous response.

Perhaps the ultimate example is that of the one we call
the 'Good Thief' (Luke 23:39–43). He admitted that his
life as a thief meant he deserved to be executed, so at
least in his own opinion his bad deeds during his lifetime
well outweighed his good deeds. On the other hand, there
was now no chance of his ever turning over a new leaf and
doing good deeds for the future, such as Zacchaeus had
promised to do. He had no time left. He was dying on a
cross. All he did was ask Jesus for forgiveness without
giving any reason at all why it should be granted. And it
was granted: 'Today you will be with me in Paradise.'

The Old Covenant was a learning process. It broke
down but God did not. St Paul points out that not all the
formulations of the Old Covenant are expressed as being
dependent on human effort: the promises to Abraham
were made without any strings attached. Among the
prophets, Jeremiah, Ezekiel and Hosea came to see that
God had a fulfilment in mind that would be unbreakable,
as turned out to be the case with the New Covenant of
Jesus. If the unchanging God has decided to love us for
no reason at all, there is absolutely nothing we can do to
break such an arrangement.

Why should the new wine destroy the old wineskins?
Why should it be dangerous to wield the New Testament
sword in an Old Testament fashion? The reason, I think,
may be clearly seen in the story of Zacchaeus. When
morality is seen from Jesus' point of view (on the 'U'
pattern instead of the doorway), the joy at being forgiven
when we do not deserve it produces a great freedom and
generosity, far beyond any strict adherence to narrow

laws. Zacchaeus was inspired to go way beyond his
duty. If his behaviour was mistakenly seen in an Old
Testament light, it could be thought that Jesus was
saying, 'Be as generous as Zacchaeus, if you want to
be saved!'

I once started to count the 'demands' or 'commands'
of Jesus in St Matthew's gospel alone, and easily reached
fifty before giving up. If all of those sayings were seen
as conditions of our being acceptable to God, we should
be in a far sorrier state than if Jesus had never come,
since they demand a far greater generosity than the Old
Testament requirements. But if instead these words of
Jesus are seen as invitations to the sinner who has
already been permanently accepted for no reason at all,
then they are an inspiration. Looked at in the 'doorway'
mode, they are an ever-heavier burden. Looked at in the
'U' mode, they are an inspiration.

Son or Daughter . . . and Servant

The belief that we are God's sons or daughters belongs
with our belief that we are God's lambs, that we are
enlightened by God, that we are only little children. All
of these images fit on what I would call the left-hand edge
of the gospel, leaving on the right-hand edge 'shepherd,
light for others, power' and now 'servant'. The letter of
St Paul to the Philippians tells us to have the same mind
that was in Christ Jesus, 'who, though he was in the
form of God, did not count equality with God a thing to
be grasped, but emptied himself, taking the form of a
servant'. As children of God we are all invited to 'partake
of the divine nature' to that extent, since anyone who
can call another 'Abba' is akin by nature to that one. So
we are called to do as Jesus our elder brother did, and
put aside the fact that we are God's children, without
however ceasing to be God's children, and to act as if
we were only servants – servants of God, that is. This
is ultimately the same as to be God's shepherd, one who
reflects God's light, or one who mediates God's power.

In the context of the Old Testament prophesies of the Servant as one who would suffer and so enter his glory, we are invited (not ordered) to keep on loving God when suffering comes our way.

We do not have to spend our lives like servants trying to deserve to be called children of God. Instead, like the Prodigal Son, we are already children of God, trying to deserve being called good servants. That son in Jesus' story (Luke 15:11–32) never ceased to be 'son', but all the way home he was planning to be a servant to his father. The titles we inherit on the left-hand edge of the Good News are such that they cannot be taken away from us.

CHAPTER 5

ROCK, FISH, COIN

Each of the frequently appearing themes of 'rock', 'fish' and 'coin' is two-edged in the gospel. The rock is first of all underneath us, then we become transformed into a rock without ceasing to be less-than-rock in ourselves. The fish is transformed into a fisher without ceasing to be fish. The coin becomes a coin-collector or a coin-seeker without ceasing to be a coin.

A useful picture is that of a stone wall being built. At the bottom is placed a firm foundation of exceptionally large stones or of cement resembling one enormous stone. Then the layers of stone are laid down. Each layer of stone, each stone, has a brief time of being totally dependent on the stones below without any responsibility for stones above. Then the stonemason comes round again and stones are placed on the free layer. So for instance we start life as children, dependent on our parents, until one day we have children and responsibilities of our own, and another layer of 'stones' comes to rest upon us.

Jesus says that without the firm foundation of his own words heard and listened to, we are like a man building a house upon sand; with his words as the foundation, we are like a man building his house on a rock. Then no matter what kind of storm or disaster hits the house, it will still stand. Once again we may use Peter 'the rock' as the clearest example. He lost everything before he realized how he was being transformed into a rock. Once he knew his own complete weakness, and that he had denied the Son of man before several men and a girl . . . and yet had been readily forgiven, then he knew that he

had the staying power of a rock. Having failed the worst
of all failures and been forgiven for it, he knew he did not
have to fear his own weakness any more, but could rely
on the forgiveness Jesus brought from his 'Abba'. He no
longer had to live up to his lofty expectations for himself;
he was no longer walking a tightrope.

The image of 'rock' slides easily into that of 'precious'
– precious metals and precious stones. So long as the
human 'rock' is firmly fixed on the divine rock of God's
forgiveness, then troubles and persecution and illness, all
the costly things, will bring the gold and the jewels out of
the human rock as well. What seemed like disaster will
turn out to be more precious than what was there before
disaster struck. The rock, like Peter, may be crushed,
but a precious and imperishable trust in God comes as
a result. The fire of the crucible reveals that which can
never be destroyed.

In the Old Testament as in the New, God is the first
Rock, totally reliable and with no foundation outside
himself. Jesus compares his own words to a rock, and St
Paul calls him the Rock. Rather like the children crossing
the road holding on to an adult's hand, we who are less
than rock-like receive the quality of rock by relying on
God's unquestioning love. Any notion that we are doing
God a favour by being good is bound to lead to disaster
once the storm comes.

What about the fish? Jesus chose several of his closest
followers from the nearby fishing community, and fishes
and fishers appear fairly frequently in the Gospels. The
two edges are: 'fish' and 'fisher'. One gets caught; the
other catches. The implication always is that only the
fish that has been caught can be turned into a fisher.
Jesus catches his disciples and then teaches them to
become fishers for him. There is always an overtone of
'baptism' where this metaphor of fish is mentioned. The
little fish are netted in the waters of baptism. Those who
go fishing for people at the call of Jesus cast their nets
wide, and those who are 'caught' are baptized. They enter
a particular area of water which is no longer the open sea,

but on the other hand they are cherished by God in a way
that was not possible before.

Even Jesus insisted on being netted in the waters of
baptism, and thus became in some sense a 'fish' before
he set about catching others as a fisher (see Matthew
3:13–17). In the early days of the Christian Church, the
'fish' sign was marked up on the doorposts of Christian
houses in times of persecution, the fish representing not
only the Christians within but also Christ. The Greek
word for 'fish' used as an acronym spelt out 'Jesus
Christ, Son of God, Saviour':

Iesous	Jesus
CHristos	Christ
THeou	of God
Uios	Son
Soter	Saviour

ICHTHUS = fish

Not so obvious is the meaning of the presence of fish in
the stories where Jesus fed large numbers of people. At
the feeding of the five thousand it was five loaves and
two fish; at the feeding of the four thousand it was seven
loaves and a few small fish. In the resurrection story of
Jesus by the lakeside in Galilee, the disciples caught
a memorable number of fish (153 – perhaps the same
number as was thought to be the number of nations in
the world), but Jesus already had fish cooking and bread
ready for their breakfast on the shore. We are not told
where Jesus got his fish from, but three times now bread
and fish are mentioned as staple food of a meal which has
overtones of the Eucharist.

I hope to show later on how bread and wine are the
food and drink of the left-hand side of the gospel and
the right-hand side, respectively. In other words, bread
feeds the child, wine is drink for the servant who suffers.
The bread that comes down from heaven feeds the child

of heaven. Those who eat the bread become one with
what they eat. By the same token those who eat the fish
become one with Christ, are fed and strengthened in their
happiness to be 'caught', and are being prepared to be
transformed along with Christ into the one who catches
many fish.

Not so clearly underlined in the gospel is the contrast
between 'coin' and 'coin-seeker', but the clues are there
nonetheless. The most obvious example is that of the
woman who lost a silver coin in her house, who lit a
lamp and swept the house and searched diligently until
she found it (Luke 15:8–10). In that chapter of Luke
where the story is told, it is placed side by side with
the story of the Lost Sheep, and the Prodigal Son, and
the joy of the searcher in each case is overflowing when
the lost one is found. The coin belonged to the woman, as
the sheep belonged to the shepherd and the son belonged
to the father.

There are other places besides where coins figure in
the Gospels. Jesus makes a lesson out of the coin that
had Caesar's head on it: since the image of Caesar
represents ownership it should be given back to Caesar.
Then Jesus says that what belongs to God should be
given back to God. It does not take much imagination
to realize that each human being is stamped with the
image of God, since we are God's children and children
bear the likeness of parents. Again it does not take
much imagination to recall that Jesus invited several
fishermen to become fishers for him, and a tax collector,
a collector of coins, to collect 'coins' for him. This does
not mean that we must pay taxes to God: Jesus says
clearly that the children of the king do not pay taxes
(Matthew 17:24–27). It means simply this: once we, coins
with God's image upon us, have been joyfully found by
the coin-seeker, on behalf of God, and collected into
his treasury, we are then called to go out and collect
others who are lost. Being found is necessary, but it
costs nothing; being a coin-seeker for God is costly, but
voluntary. Those who try to collect the children with

God's image may easily be seen as tax collectors, and
share in the tax collector's unpopularity.

Whilst on the subject of money and God and unpopularity, we may ask why God was so unpopular in the
story of the talents (Matthew 25:14–30) or the pounds
(Luke 19:11–27)? God is represented by the man who
gives out the money to the three characters. Two are
successful in their trading, but the other takes no risks
and is condemned for taking no risks. 'I knew you to be
a hard man, . . . so I was afraid', he pleads. If we are
running away from God, we see only darkness, and we
do not see that God is incurably friendly. Hence if the
Truth appears to be unfriendly, it must pay to play safe.
The one in the dark is like someone walking a tightrope,
afraid to make a mistake and giving an impression of God
as a hard taskmaster.

The ones who see God as utterly friendly and helpful,
on the other hand, know they have nothing to lose.
They grow to be generous, just as we saw in the case
of Zacchaeus. God is not hard or mean or grasping
or demanding, but if we convince ourselves that he
is like that, then for one thing we are worshipping
a false god, and for another thing we are distorting
reality, and reality will not be distorted. For those who
know themselves to be now and forever lambs of God,
enlightened, little children, sons and daughters of God,
there is nothing to fear in the parable of the talents.

CHAPTER 6

ONE SEED AND MANY

One of the most consoling thoughts that ever came to me was this: if the world were an island, and everyone in the world sailed away in a large liner leaving me behind, where would Jesus be? He would be still on the island with me, since as long as they did it to the least of his little ones, they did it to him. When we put the Good News round the right way, with lambs coming first and shepherds only afterwards, it is each single human being that matters before the whole human race.

In the Old Testament, we get a distinct impression that it is the people as a whole that matters, and individuals had better keep up or they will be left behind. The Old Covenant is written and built up as a blueprint for a perfect community, and people who do not fit will get left out. Another effect of Jesus' use of family metaphors for his community is that nobody gets left behind. In our own day, if a family went on an afternoon walk in the hills, and the littlest one began to be weary, the attitude of mother or father is always, 'The family is not home until we are all home'. There is never any question of leaving the little one on the hillside and everyone else hurrying to be home in time for supper!

The oldest version of the Lord's Prayer, Luke's version (Luke 11:1–4) does not say 'Our Father' but simply 'Father'. I find this, too, consoling, because if everyone sailed away and left me behind, I could still cry 'Father' and be heard, whereas I would be feeling too deserted to cry 'Our Father', since I would no longer be one of 'us'. Quite honestly, I would regard a salvation that saved everyone else and left me out as no salvation at all. St Paul apparently toyed with the idea of offering himself as a hostage or a victim: 'I could wish that I myself were accursed' if that would bring Christ to his fellow Israelites, but he says that, knowing such a sacrifice to be out of the question (see Romans 9:1–5).

So it is that we find Jesus going round the fringes of society and picking up the ones who do not fit the orthodox pattern. He looked for the blind, the deaf, the lame, the paralysed, the lepers, and those with mental disorders; women were pushed to the fringes of society as well, so he has a special care for every woman. He came to call sinners, such as could not cope with the forest of decrees and ordinances that had grown up – and not only those who were caught in legal mazes, but also straightforward sinners such as thieves and adulterers.

As the Good Shepherd he 'called each one by name'. There is far more in the Gospels about Jesus spending time healing individuals than there is about his healing of crowds; and even when he is said to have healed many people, there is nothing to say he did not heal them one at a time.

The very pattern of Christianity in its beginnings shows the importance of the one before the many. Jesus knew himself to be the *one* Son of God and knew himself to be called to share this way of looking at God with the rest of the human race. One man died to save the people, it was not the people who died to save one man. One Shepherd died for the sheep, it was not the sheep who died to save one shepherd. I owe my salvation not to any real or supposed keeping of Christian moral rules, but to the fact that Jesus died rather than let me be left behind.

It is a while now since I referred to the two-edged sword of the gospel, or to the way in which each half is divided again. Following the 'sword' image, we may say that a two-edged sword has two edges indeed, but also two flat sides to the blade. The other image I suggested was that of a symphony with four movements which falls into

two clear halves. God loves; I trust. God calls; I come.
The seed parables of Jesus fit very neatly into the four
movements. The sower sows the seed, which falls on the
ground. That is the first movement. The ground opens
up and hides the seed in the dark for a while. That is
the second movement. The seed starts to grow out into
the light. That is the third movement. The seed becomes
fruitful and produces thirty, sixty, one hundred times
its own self: it becomes a sower. That is the fourth
movement.

The seed is the Word of God, which in the New
Covenant is telling us we are loved because we are God's
children, not because we are good children. If we can open
our hearts and take in the Good News, then our salvation
is assured. It does not cost us anything; we do not have to
do anything apart from believe. The perfect example, as
I have already pointed out, is the man we call the 'Good
Thief'. He took the Good News into his heart, and was
promised that it would be fruitful in Paradise. Certainly
his story has been endlessly fruitful in encouraging the
near-hopeless to trust in God's kindness even when
reason would say it is too late.

Most people who welcome the Good News from God into
their hearts do not then die very soon afterwards. Life
goes on. Inevitably there is a reaction to the goodness
God has shown, and the one who has heard the news
wants to respond by doing something to please God, even
to alter the whole pattern of their life to please God. The
Light calls them to grow. And if they answer the call,
the desire, to please God then they begin to live fruitful
lives, fruitful especially in persuading others to believe
in God's goodness. This of course is best done by living a
compassionate life in imitation of God's way, and this in
turn may lead to suffering, since the compassionate are
often exploited.

Under the image of the two-edged sword, I would
picture the two edges as the movements that come
immediately from God. God sows the seed; God as the
light draws or invites the little plant to grow. The

'cutting' of the cutting edges may be thought of like this: I cannot cut away my pride so that the ground of my heart opens up to the idea of being a little child, a mere nothing, a lamb. Only God can penetrate my heart like that, and make what before seemed like folly into the most beautiful truth ever seen. And for the other cutting edge, Jesus' way of the cross is the way the young plant is called to grow, but it is Jesus' call and inspiration that makes it possible. His burden is light, because he has already shown us that we do not have to succeed. There is no competition, no risk. If we die no more fruitful than the Good Thief, we will have done very well.

Weeds

The seed which is the Word of God comes from above ground, sown by God who is 'from above', in Jesus' expression. Love which is unconditional comes only from somewhere beyond human limits. The progress of the seed which is God's Word follows the 'U' pattern, not the pattern of the 'doorway' which is the other way up. The weeds that Jesus speaks of in some of his parables, on the other hand, must follow the doorway pattern, starting with the earth, coming 'from below', and not being planted by God. To his enemies Jesus says, 'You are from below; I am from above' (John 8:23). In another place Jesus apparently compares the weeds to 'the cares of the world, and the delight in riches, and the desire for other things' (Mark 4:19). The fruits they produce are not useful.

The strongest parable about weeds is the one about the farmer who sowed good seed in his field, only to find an enemy had sown darnel (weeds), as well. There are two ways of taking that parable and Jesus' given explanation of it (Matthew 13:24–30). One is the blunt way, which Jesus would use for those running away from God, meaning that those who turn their backs on God face destruction. The other is the gentler way, bearable for those who are facing God and trying to keep facing God,

meaning that the field is myself, with good fruits growing
and weeds growing; God who is ever-forgiving wishes me
to keep on producing the good, and he will deliver me
from the evil at the end. Any good teacher knows that
to concentrate on the pupils' faults exclusively destroys
their incentive to carry on trying, whereas to praise and
encourage the good leads to a far greater fruitfulness in
the subject.

CHAPTER 7

GUIDED BECOMES GUIDE

B efore ever Christians were called Christians, they were called Followers of the Way. And the Way was already thought of as the Way of the cross, or the Way through the cross to glory. Simon of Cyrene was remembered both as himself, the father of Alexander and Rufus, but also as a symbol of the Christian life, carrying the cross alongside Jesus so as to share in his glory. Jesus called himself the Way, and spent two or three years inducting his chosen disciples, leading them in his way so that they in turn would be able to lead others as he had led them. Here we have another image which parallels the 'lamb and shepherd', the 'enlightened and lighting' and all the rest, saying almost the same things but with a different picture.

The four movements of the symphony under the image of the Way go like this. First, Jesus finds a lost and broken traveller – the first movement. Then, the traveller lets himself or herself be cared for and mended by Jesus. Already all is well for the traveller. That is the second movement. The third movement comes when Jesus invites the traveller, now definitely on the mend, to come with him along the road: it is an understood thing that if they meet any other wounded travellers they will not walk on by unconcerned. 'Go and do likewise' is the conclusion of the parable of the Good Samaritan (Luke 10:37). It may not immediately occur to the traveller that Jesus will travel alongside, so the traveller may ask, 'How can I know where we are going, since I myself do not know the way?' But once Jesus gives an assurance that he will come too, then the traveller is inspired to say, 'Yes, now I will come, since you call me'.

Again, moving over to the image of the two-edged sword, the cutting edges belong to God, and they are kindly. God's Word penetrates the wounded traveller, like oil and wine on the wounds, and gives the confidence to trust God's help offered through Jesus. Jesus, in promising to accompany the mended traveller on the Way of the cross, encourages the traveller to trust that all will be well. Swords, however, have to be treated with the greatest respect, if they are not to cut the unwary. For someone totally unwilling to be helped by God, the sword seems like an avenging sword. One whose back is turned on God imagines that the sword is coming in pursuit, and such a one runs away all the harder down the road away from God instead of towards God. Then the Way of the cross can only feel like an impossible burden, so many 'commands' before this implacable God is satisfied – definitely not worth turning round for. 'And what has this God ever done for me?' is the next complaint.

Saint Ignatius Loyola has an illustration which may well be useful here. Anyone whose back is firmly turned against God will find that evil deeds beckon him on, whereas God is a constant reproach and goad at his back. However, once the person has turned round and faced God, and found that God has never ceased being loving and forgiving, then good deeds begin to beckon him on, and evil becomes a temptation at his back.[1] There is one road, in other words, and it all depends which way we are facing, whether the two-edged sword works for our good or for our harm. God cannot cease to be good, nor can he cease to be welcoming from where he is at the end of the road, but if we turn our backs we interpret the vacuum we face as being ill-will on God's part.

The consolation then is, if we can but listen to it, that no matter how far we have run away from God, all is immediately well as soon as we turn round and face God, since God is still smiling, still looking with love, and distance is no object with an infinite lover. We do

not have to improve before God will love us: that would be
to take God's measure once again from the Old Covenant.
If God is 'from above' and the road is stretching upwards
towards God, then the first move comes from above, when
God sends rescue down to the traveller. If the traveller,
who was facing the wrong way and lost, lets the rescuer
turn him gently round to face the right way, then the
traveller begins to have the courage to climb thereafter
towards God, in the right direction, and with a heart full
of gratitude. Any, on the other hand, whose sights are set
determinedly on succeeding 'from below', by their own
efforts, will find in the end that they are only pursuing
emptiness.

Jesus' Way to me, when he came to rescue me, was
not easy by human standards, though he called it easy.
I suppose a difficult thing done for someone we love
becomes easier the more we love the other. But being
rescued was incredibly easy. Once it became clear to
me that God is endlessly forgiving, seventy times seven
times in the day and beyond, then all the load of guilt and
shame and confusion was wiped away, never to return
except as an ineffectual temptation. Jesus in effect said
to his contemporaries about each one of us in human
history, 'I stake my life on the fact that God loves each
one with an everlasting love'. In effect, he refused to sail
away and leave me behind, no matter what I had done,
so long as I wanted to be with him and was willing to be
with the rest of us sinners.

Jesus says that if we want to be disciples of his, we
must take up the cross each day. What he does *not* say,
is that in order to be *saved* we have to take up the cross.
Jesus took up his cross to save us; we are invited to take
up our cross to join with him, as disciples, to share in the
saving of others. 'Many' are saved, and all of those saved
are invited or called to go on to be disciples. The number
who actually become disciples is few. There are inevitably
many more sheep, hundreds or thousands more, than
there are shepherds. For the many who are unwilling to
go through the narrow door, there are just a few willing

to go through. But the few, along with Jesus, are those who save the many through their unity with Jesus. One shepherd dies to save his thousand sheep, he does not die to save himself. So too the 'few' who are 'chosen' are chosen to help in the saving of the many; they are not chosen to be an exclusive club in heaven, leaving everyone else outside.

I am sure the reason why the gospel appears to be sometimes frightening and sometimes sublimely consoling has something to do with Jesus' awareness of the way his listeners were facing, either towards God or away from God. I have mentioned already the parable of the field with corn and weeds, which can either be paralysingly stern or greatly encouraging, depending on whether we are running away from God or facing up the road towards him. Another such story is that of the shepherd separating the sheep from the goats (Matthew 25:31–46). The stern interpretation designed, I am sure, to be a goad to anyone running away from God, would be that the Son of man at the end of the world will divide all the good people from all the bad people for ever. The kindly interpretation would notice that very few, if any, are totally bad in the terms that Jesus describes, or totally good either. I may have 'fed the hungry' somewhat by sharing the wonders of the gospel with those who could not see it as beautiful; but what about all those literally hungry people whom I have not fed? I may have visited many sick people, but there were many more I could have visited and did not. Prison visiting has not been much of a feature in my life. Some strangers I have welcomed, some I have run away from. So where does that leave me, as a sheep? or as a goat? I suspect most of us are a mixture. Jesus' parable is a constant reminder of the things that matter, the actions that have an eternal value. He is constantly inviting us to go for them, and leave aside the selfish ambitions. At the end he will separate the good in each of us from the evil in each of us, and only the good will go on to eternal life.

In summary, then, the two edges of the sword in this

case of 'the Way' are first, 'guided' and second, 'guide';
first 'shown how' and second 'showing others how'. First
I observe, even while it is happening, the way Jesus saves
me, forgives me, will not leave me behind. Then I am
invited to show the same compassion to anyone else I
pass along the road.

CHAPTER 8

WAITED ON AND SERVANT

T he time has come to extend the list started on page 9. As before, the 'passive' and more essential features from the gospel are on the left, the 'active' and voluntary on the right. These then are further characteristics of the two edges of the gospel:

waited on by God	servant/slave
Mary	Martha
Jesus baptized by John	Jesus transfigured
baptism	confirmation
bread and water	wine
free	costly
forgiven	forgiving
'You are my beloved'	'This is my beloved . . . listen to him/her'
Spirit loves	Spirit calls (invites)
faith the response	love the response
necessary	voluntary
water	fire

First, then, to consider the contrast between 'being waited on by God' and 'being invited to be a servant or a slave'. The fundamental one of the two is 'being waited on by God'. We have already touched on the special meaning attached to 'Servant' when it is applied to Jesus as the fulfilment of the prophecies. There the word implies a willingness to lay down one's life not just for friends but for enemies as well. Since this is thought of as being the culmination of the idea of 'servant', it will

be as well to review why the death of Jesus was a service
to the rest of the human race, and why the death of a
Christian can be redemptive with and in Christ.

Jesus came 'from above', bringing from God that
which can only come from God, namely unconditional
forgiveness and love. He came with a message of love
and forgiveness for every single human being, no matter
how few qualifications the creature had or has for being
forgiven. Those who were tied up by guilt welcomed him
and his message, and recognized it as being from God.
Those who did not believe in forgiveness but preferred to
stand before God on their own merits did not accept Jesus.
He was successful, and so successful that his enemies
insisted that he cease from his teaching, or they would
have him killed.

Jesus in the Garden of Gethsemane had a choice. He
could either run away back to Nazareth or to somewhere
even more obscure, and stop preaching, or he could
insist on his message and face certain death. There
passed in the garden the final hours in which he was
free to choose. If he had backed down, he would have
been untrue to his Abba, who would, we must surely
believe, have forgiven him. He would have been untrue
also to all the poor sinners and outcasts to whom he
had given such hope. He would have been saying in
effect, 'Forget my message; it is costing me too much.
Perhaps God loves you up to a point, but there are
limits'. In holding to his message Jesus was true to
his Father and true to the likes of me, since I certainly
do not expect or hope to enter the kingdom on my
own merits.

For the disciples, the two great joys of the resurrection
were, first, that Jesus was alive and well, and second,
that Jesus was *right*. So Jesus had put their interests
ahead of his own immediate interests, and as such Jesus
had behaved like a servant. This was something only
Jesus could do, with his Father's blessing. If anyone else
had died for the truth of God's unbreakable love ... well,
could anyone else have dared to die for that without the

authority Jesus brought, and without the reassurance of
the Resurrection to show he was right?

Thus God's service to humankind comes first, through
Jesus. Under God's inspiration, humans may follow in
Jesus' footsteps, but only if he served us first. A beautiful
illustration of this truth may be found in John's account
of the Last Supper. Jesus put aside his garments, girded
himself with a towel, poured water in a basin, and
began to wash the disciples' feet, wiping them dry with
the towel. This was a servant's task, but when Peter
objected and said, 'You shall never wash my feet', Jesus
replied, 'If I do not wash you, you have no part in me'.
So Peter willingly, more than willingly, let Jesus serve
him. After the lesson Jesus said to them, 'I have given
you an example, that you also should do as I have done
to you'. Like a vine with its branches, the original stock
is followed by smaller branches which are one with the
vine. There is one vine, with many branches; there is one
Servant, with many lesser sevants. Now that the truth
is out, about God's unconditional love, more than one
person may die for that truth, as a gift of trust in God
and as an inspiration to other human beings.

Being served and being a servant is not only about
dying. God serves us in so many ordinary ways, and
we are invited to serve God in so many ordinary, simple,
ways. I hesitate to say first of all that we are called to
serve one another: we are, of course, but we are called
to serve God first. Jesus told his disciples that they were
to serve one another and the whole human race, but that
evidently did not mean doing whatever anyone else chose
to command. Jesus was a servant to his enemies: but
Jesus did not change his message at the bidding of his
enemies. So too we should not feel obliged to lose our own
integrity in order to suit someone else's expressed needs,
and indeed we should think carefully before sacrificing
our health and wellbeing for someone else, making quite
sure this is a greater good than the alternative.

Jesus insists many times that his disciples should not
compete for the top places in this life (e.g. Mark 9:33–37).

They should never forget that they are to be like little
children, drawing all their power from God and not from
their own resources. A leader in the kingdom will be one
who has experienced being lifted from nothing by God,
and who therefore does not put on airs. The very fact of
being humble before God will make the person a leader
in the kingdom, since such behaviour encourages the
weak and helpless to come and join the movement:
they are children of God and as such are as valuable
as anybody else. Competition for the highest places only
perpetuates the spirit of 'earning heaven' which Jesus
came to reverse.

Jesus' speeches and sayings are full of reminders that
God is, was and will always be at our service. God is the
heavenly Father who feeds the birds and counts every
hair on our heads. He clothes the flowers in magnificence;
he will care for his children. He promises eternal life to
those willing to take it as a gift. God loves and forgives
us for no reason at all, and for ever; we are invited to
believe ourselves his children. No one is so insignificant,
so sick, so sinful, as to be outside God's care.

'When you have done all that is commanded you, say,
"We are unworthy servants; we have only done what was
our duty."' (Luke 17:10). In saying that, Jesus makes
it clear that our service is not a means of earning
heaven, of earning eternal life. Our service belongs on
the right-hand side of the two edges of the gospel, as a
grateful response to the service God has already given
to us. Our service is secondary; God's service through
Jesus is fundamental. Just as a child becomes powerful
when holding tight to an adult crossing the road, so a
poor person whom God has served and saved becomes a
powerful servant so long as the link of humility is there
with God.

One sword, two edges and two sides. One symphony,
two halves, four movements. First movement: God is, was
and always will be at our service. Second movement: a
human being accepts that all of life is a gift. First half,
therefore, equals 'being served'. Third movement: the

invitation comes to each of us, to give and serve as we
have been served. Fourth movement: the invitation is
taken up, without fear over likely or possible failure, since
the service is a privilege, not a condition of salvation.
Second half, therefore, equals 'our service'. Within the
'sword' image, the first edge is God's service, the first
side, our recognition of the service; the second edge is
God's invitation through Jesus, to serve in gratitude, the
second side of the blade is our response.

Mary and Martha

As a final example of the priority of 'being served' over
'service', we may take a brief look at the story of the
woman named Martha who received Jesus into her house
(Luke 10:38–42). She had a sister called Mary, who sat at
the Lord's feet and listened to his teaching. 'But Martha
was distracted with much serving; and she went to him
and said, "Lord, do you not care that my sister has left
me to serve alone? Tell her then to help me." But the
Lord answered her, "Martha, Martha, you are anxious
and troubled about many things; one thing is needful.
Mary has chosen the good portion, which shall not be
taken away from her."' Mary here was making sure
she had heard what Jesus had to say, before jumping
in and deciding for herself what was necessary. In terms
of some of the other images we have looked at, Mary was
making sure she knew how the Shepherd rescued her,
before trying to rescue others; she was absorbing the
Light, before trying to shine herself; she was becoming
like a little child, before attempting to link with anyone
else across a dangerous road. What is more, the gift
she had chosen would never be taken from her, since
the lamb becomes a shepherd without ceasing to be a
lamb; the dark surface becomes a light without ceasing
to be dependent on the light itself; the child becomes
powerful without ceasing to be weak in itself. Mary's
time will come to serve, but by then she will know what
she is about.

CHAPTER 9

JESUS BAPTIZED;
JESUS TRANSFIGURED

The Gospels of Matthew, Mark and Luke all relate the stories of Jesus' baptism at the start of his ministry, and of his transfiguration round about the time he began to make his final journey to Jerusalem. Mark is the most consistent in making the connections between these two events and what follows in each case in the gospel story, I shall spend more time looking at his gospel later. But the baptism of Jesus and the transfiguration will serve very well to show how the Synoptic Gospels each demonstrate what I have called the two edges of the gospel.

The first edge, as we have seen, is the edge that makes a man, woman or child into God's lamb, into the one on whom the light of God's love shines, a little child, a son or a daughter, built on a rock, a little fish caught in God's net, a coin with God's image upon it, a field sown with God's seed, one who is shown the way, one who is not impatient but listens first to what God has to say. The baptism of Jesus fits him into this category quite clearly at the beginning of his ministry.

John's Gospel is the one in which John the Baptist calls Jesus the Lamb at the time of the baptism (John 1:29). The voice from heaven in Mark and Luke is the voice of the Father, and speaks directly to Jesus, saying, 'You are my beloved Son; with you I am well pleased.' Jesus willingly listens, just as he had willingly entered the 'net' of baptism. The first two movements of the 'symphony' are there: first, God's unconditional love, then Jesus' free acceptance of it. I say 'unconditional' because God's

statements are eternal: God is not 'well pleased' today
and 'displeased' tomorrow. Jesus will never cease to be
God's beloved.

The transfiguration of Jesus, on the other hand, clearly
belongs with the other half of the symphony, the other
edge of the sword. There the gospel images we have
seen to be: shepherd, light for others, power, servant,
rock for others, fisher, coin seeker, sower, guide, worker.
Matthew and Mark place the transfiguration just after
Jesus has begun to speak plainly about his intention to go
to Jerusalem and about the death he will undergo there.
Luke places the story as the last event before Jesus sets
out on his Jerusalem journey. The setting is that of the
Shepherd who will lay down his life for his sheep, of the
Servant who puts God's desire to save the human race
before his own interests, indeed before his own life. Here
the power of God shines through Jesus, who is normally
as gentle as a child. It is the power to speak up for who
he is, even under threat of death. Because his death is
redemptive, it is the supreme act of the one who is a
fisher, a coin-seeker, a rock for others, a fruitful plant
or tree. The unconditional love for sinners which his
death will show is a light reflecting the unconditional
love of God.

This time there are witnesses, Peter, James and John
whom Jesus brought up the mountain with him. The
cloud around Jesus puts us in mind of the Holy Spirit,
since it parallels the vision of the dove descending on
Jesus in his baptism. The cloud is also associated with
the coming of the Son of man with power and glory. This
time the voice from heaven does not speak directly to
Jesus, but to the witnesses: 'This is my beloved Son;
listen to him.' At first sight, that is simply a command
to the witnesses to listen; but implicitly it is an invitation
to Jesus to speak up. In the circumstances, the voice from
heaven amounts to an invitation to Jesus to put his life
at risk, something which was not obviously included in
the words spoken from heaven at the baptism.

Soon it becomes clear that there is a second gift

involved here, which only God can give and which must be prayed for. All three Synoptic Gospels run the story of the transfiguration directly into the story of the epileptic boy who, at times, in a crisis, could not speak. The disciples could not heal the boy. According to Mark, Jesus tells them that this kind of dumb and deaf demon can only be cast out by prayer. Prayer is also needed to enable someone to speak up in a crisis. Sure enough, on the night of Jesus' arrest, he prayed for three hours in great personal anguish but was then able to speak up for who he was at his trial that night and the next morning. Peter and the others, on the other hand, did not pray along with Jesus, and Peter was then struck dumb, in effect, when challenged about his connection with Jesus.

For a lost lamb to become a found and loved lamb, one gift is needed: God's unconditional love. For a found and loved lamb to become a shepherd, a second gift is needed to work the marvel. And it is a gift that has to be prayed for: the gift of witnessing before the world who I am in the sight of God, when the world will not believe me. Likewise there is a second gift needed for a dark surface to become a light, for a child to become powerful, for a son or daughter to act as a servant, for corruptible stone to become precious stone, for a fish to become a fisher, for a coin to become a coin-seeker, for earth to become fertile, for a blind person to become a true guide. The very images that Jesus uses make it plain that a special gift is required, to go on from one edge of the gospel to the other.

The two-edged Gospel of Mark

The whole idea of a two-edged gospel, and also of the four movements of the 'symphony' which is the gospel, came to me from studying the Gospel of Mark. I have already written a book about Mark's gospel, incorporating my ideas about the two halves and the four quarters of that Gospel, so I shall only summarize here.[1] Perhaps the

most immediately striking evidence for Mark's Gospel
being composed of two halves is the way the sufferings
of Jesus do not get mentioned until halfway through,
when Mark says that Jesus *began* to teach his closest
disciples that the Son of man must suffer many things.
'And he said this plainly' (8:31–32). Before then, there
has been opposition and Jesus has made enemies, but
there is no talk of the cross, or of the Way of Jesus as
ending up by way of a cross. Jesus speaks of himself
in one passage as 'the bridegroom' who will be taken
away from the wedding guests, but the reference there
to his sufferings is very veiled. There seem to me to be
four clear quarters in Mark's Gospel. The first quarter
contains the baptism of Jesus, his early ministry, the
opposition he raised in Galilee, and many healings: of
a woman with fever, of a leper, of a man with a withered
hand, of a paralytic, of men who were possessed, of a
woman with a haemorrhage, and lastly he raised Jairus'
daughter from the dead. Also within that quarter come
the parables about the sower sowing seed, and how the
seed stays in the dark before coming out into the light to
be fruitful. The message is all about the message as such,
rather than the content of the message: Jesus simply asks
people to listen, to be healed, to turn back to God.

   To my mind, the key to the message itself is in the
words from heaven spoken to Jesus at his baptism: 'You
are my beloved Son; with you I am well pleased'. Within
the same quarter of the gospel Jesus is already calling
anyone who does the will of God (and therefore, anyone
who *listens*), his own brother and sister. So the words of
God may be applied to anyone who is baptized and listens
to Jesus. At this stage, to listen means simply to accept
God's adoption: no other response is yet asked for. God's
unconditional love is announced for whoever will accept
it. 'You are my beloved son; with you I am well pleased',
and equally 'You are my beloved daughter; with you I
am well pleased'.

   The second quarter of the Gospel of Mark also has no
references to Jesus' death, or mention of the cross for

his followers. In it Jesus shows himself as the Shepherd promised by God, feeding the sheep on the green grass by the quiet waters till they are satisfied: it shows Jesus the prophet like Moses feeding the people in the desert. It shows the contrast between the Shepherd-King that is Jesus and the false shepherd-king that is Herod; it shows the contrast between Jesus' teaching and that of the Pharisees and some of the scribes, also false shepherds. Above all, throughout the first half of the Gospel but especially in the second quarter, we are shown Jesus working patiently, and even urgently at times, to open up the hearts of his disciples to let his message in, and to see who he really is. Can they see that his message is from God and therefore to be trusted absolutely?

Peter eventually sees and answers 'You are the Christ', and from then on the nature of the Gospel changes radically. All the Gospel, up to this crucial answer of Peter, has belonged fair and square with what I have called the first edge of the gospel, or the first two movements of the symphony which is the gospel. It is all about God's unconditional love, and being children of God, and lambs, and sown with seed, and all the rest of the images on the left-hand side of my double list. Martha and Mary are not mentioned in this Gospel of Mark, but the first half is definitely about Mary's portion, rather than about Martha's hard work.

The third quarter of Mark's Gospel takes the story from Jesus' first prediction of the Passion down to the entry into Jerusalem for what we know (largely thanks to Mark's arrangement of the days) as Holy Week. Jesus is invited by the voice from heaven to speak out for who he is in spite of lethal opposition; the disciples are invited by Jesus to follow, even though they will not be able to respond until Jesus' work is done. We notice that Jesus had already set his mind on going to Jerusalem before the transfiguration occurred, as if the vision there was more for the benefit of the witnesses than for Jesus himself. It is noticeable also how during the third quarter of the Gospel Jesus makes a straight journey to Jerusalem, whereas in the first half of the Gospel his journeys took him in many varied directions.[2] He almost seems to have waited and waited for an assertion of faith, made eventually by Peter, and then decided he was safe to face his destiny. The message had sunk in, and would in time be fruitful.

As Jesus makes his way to Jerusalem, he is inviting his disciples to follow him, and do as he does. A disciple must take up the cross, a disciple must aim for the lowest place, a disciple must be prepared to give up earthly riches, a disciple must be prepared to leave family connections, a disciple must welcome the little ones. A disciple must identify with a blind beggar, and acknowledge that without the power and vision from God, the whole Way of Jesus will seem like nonsense, so the power must be prayed for earnestly.

The fourth quarter of Mark's Gospel is the story of Holy Week, and the suffering, death and resurrection of Jesus. The Shepherd lays down his life for his sheep, Jesus' words and actions are a light to the world, the power of God shines through and is seen even by the centurion who executed Jesus, the Servant suffers and so enters his glory, the seed of God dies and is fruitful. God's invitation to Jesus expressed at the transfiguration is generously taken up by Jesus at his trial; also the need for prayer at this stage is recognized. Whereas the grace of being forgiven, early on in the Gospel, could be given even when the sinner had never asked for it, the power to love God in return has to be prayed for, as the price is sometimes high and we are only beggars.

In the first half of Mark's Gospel, bread and water were many times in evidence. Jesus went often to, and across, the lake of Galilee, and there was frequent mention of bread and other food. Jesus was too busy to eat: his friends thought he was beside himself to be so careless of his own needs. The little girl raised from the dead was hungry and Jesus gave instructions that she be given something to eat. Next we hear of Herod's banquet for his birthday, and by contrast the simple meal Jesus gave to the thousands on the hill, beside the waters of the lake. Then the four thousand are fed. Then there is anxiety about there being only one loaf on the boat. Bread and fish and water. In the second half of the Gospel, the bread reappears, at the Passover meal on the night Jesus was arrested. Wine is identified by Jesus with his sufferings, in his encounter with James and John over 'the cup that I drink', and also wine is there at the Passover supper: 'This is my blood of the new covenant'. I will leave a discussion of the reasons why bread, water and fish belong with the first edge of the gospel, and wine with bread belongs to the second edge, until a later chapter, but simply note here the way in which not just blood, but wine as well, as a symbol of suffering, is left to the second half of Mark's Gospel.

A final observation about Mark's Gospel concerns the interwoven stories of the withering of the fig tree and the cleansing of the temple, during the early days of Holy Week. The fig tree looked beautiful and fruitful, but was not: it was not the season for figs. Therefore, with a surprising logic, Jesus shows the tree as doomed to wither. The temple too looked beautiful, splendid, and was supposed to be fruitful. But here was the Son of the owner coming for fruit and catching the temple 'out of season', unfruitful as far as God was concerned. No purely human institution, no institution that starts from the ground and expects to reach heaven, can ultimately succeed. Unless the gift comes from heaven first, the tree and the temple will never be able to be fruitful at all seasons. We are back with the difference between the 'doorway' approach to God, and the everlastingly fruitful 'U' approach that starts from God's inexhaustible love.

CHAPTER 10

BAPTISM AND CONFIRMATION

T he first fact to be acknowledged in writing a chapter about baptism and confirmation is that many Christians do not recognize or celebrate a sacrament of confirmation, and many of those that do, feel they could well do without it. What I hope to do in these few pages is to show how well such a celebration fits in with the images of the gospel we have been looking at. Therefore I would hope to encourage those who do celebrate confirmation, to see how it fits in with the Gospels; and to encourage those who celebrate baptism but not confirmation as a sacrament, to keep separate the truth of adoption as God's children, which comes first, and the invitation to do great things for God, which comes second and is voluntary. This should be possible, especially in the case of the baptism of adults.

Newly-baptized Christians need time to absorb the fact that they are God's lambs, enlightened by God, and possessors of all the titles I have collected on the left-hand side of my double list. More importantly, they need to celebrate God's unconditional love *before* getting that love confused with their own response of love. Otherwise the newly baptized may feel they are taking on a burden greater than that expected of the people of the Old Testament. 'Grace' will help them, to be sure, but the essential grace is the realization of God's unquestioning love, and if that has not been allowed to take root, how can it help anybody? The gospel writers themselves are well aware of the continuity between the seed that is sown and the fruitful plant that grows as a result of

the sowing. But I think I have shown quite thoroughly,
if simply, that there has to be a radical change of
direction between one edge and the other of the living
gospel, between the first half and the second half of the
'symphony'. Faith and trust will always grow into love,
given time and opportunity, but when the opportunity or
the time is not there, then faith or trust is enough – as
is clear from the story of the Good Thief. Why this point
is so essential is that only when a newly-baptized person
realizes that faith or trust is enough, only then will he
or she find the freedom of heart to produce good works,
works of eternal value. Good works done on that basis
are divine, since there is no selfish calculation in them
at all. They are simply done in gratitude. Their source is
in God, and in nothing else.

The rite for the baptism of infants and young children
makes it clear that the sacrament belongs entirely with
the first edge of the two-edged gospel. The child is rejoiced
over as a child of God: we should remember that the
sacrament celebrates a fact that is already true. Just
as a wedding anniversary means so much less if one or
other partner to the marriage forgets to mark the date,
and yet the anniversary is still an anniversary, so a child
of God is a child of God even if nobody celebrates, but
the celebration brings home the happiness of the truth.
Water is used for the baptism, and the meaning of the
symbolism is spelled out. Water creates; waters of the
flood cleansed the earth for new life to grow; water made
a barrier to leave the slavery of Egypt behind; Jesus'
baptism by John, in the Jordan, was the model for our
baptism; water and blood flowed from the side of Christ
in the act of our redemption.

The child is usually given a white garment, or else
comes already clothed in white. What we need to remember here is that the 'inner' garment is thenceforth white
for ever. We do not put dirty marks on our baptismal robe
by sinning later on. That robe stands for God calling the
child 'my beloved', and such a relationship remains for
ever. Beauty is in the eye of the beholder, and if God calls

that child 'my beloved' then that child is lovable, now and forever. God does not shift and change. The child is also given a lighted candle, lighted from the paschal candle which represents the risen Christ. There is no suggestion as yet that the child will have to hold up the light some day, so as to give light to everyone else in the house. That will come, but not yet, not in the context of baptism alone. Near the end of the rite, there is a prayer over the ears and mouth of the child, which corresponds nicely to the '*Ephphatha*' prayer of Jesus in the first half of Mark's Gospel (see Mark 7:34). The desire and intention of the prayer is that the child will in time hear how much God loves him or her, and will be able to praise God for such goodness. The mouth is not yet blessed for witnessing to God's love before an unbelieving world.

The rite for the baptism of children is composed of such elements not just because the ones to be baptized are children, and therefore not yet capable of responding actively. These aspects belong with the very nature of baptism. The gospel model for the Church's sacrament of baptism is the baptism of Jesus, at least the version written by St Mark and St Luke. According to these two, the voice from heaven said to Jesus, 'You are my beloved', rather than, 'This is my beloved', as St Matthew has it. Baptism is an affair between God and the one to be baptized: the witnesses are only watching. The candidate is not called upon to witness either. The dove in all three Synoptic Gospels is a sign of the presence of the Holy Spirit, and a reminder of the dove that returned to the ark of Noah bringing an olive branch. God's anger is over, new life is growing. In fact, God's anger never was: anger is what happens when God is not there, but now at last the realization of the truth is available to the human race. Forgiveness is seen to be available for the asking. The one being baptized was chosen by God before the foundation of the world and is beloved by God. That love is there today and will be there for ever. There are no conditions. All the candidate has to do is to accept the love and trust in it. The love

comes of being God's child and not from some successful
performance.

The obvious gospel model for the sacrament of confirmation is I believe to be found in the transfiguration of
Jesus. Jesus does not cease to be beloved in the transfiguration: all three Gospels of Matthew, Mark and Luke
agree that the voice said 'This is my Son, the Beloved'.
Just as the lamb becomes a shepherd without ceasing to
be a lamb, so Jesus becomes the lover without ceasing to
be beloved. Thus too God's child is called and invited to
become God's servant without ceasing to be God's child.
It could be said (in fact I have said this many, many
times), what is really celebrated in confirmation is that
God through the minister is saying *to the congregation*
about the candidate, 'This is my beloved son; listen to
him', or, 'This is my beloved daughter; listen to her'.
And what the candidate is there being invited to do is
to speak up: to speak up for being God's child, a sinner
but forgiven. Serious prayer is needed this time, and
from now on prayer by the candidate not just others.
From now on the candidate is invited to love others in
God's way, for no reason except that they ask for love or
need it. The one being confirmed is invited to love without
expecting any return for that love; only from God is love
for the candidate guaranteed. Failures in the candidate's
love for others will, of course, be forgiven that instant, so
that the candidate may try again with a good heart.

In baptism God is not expecting anything in return.
That is the nature of God's love. There is no question of
God's ever cancelling baptism because of poor response.
He gives a gift, a total gift of himself. God is whole and
entire wherever he is, so we do not possess part of God,
we are given the whole of God. Each of us has God's
undivided attention all the time and for all time and
eternity. I look out through my eyes and see what
nobody else in the whole world can see – the world
through my eyes – and yet God sees what I see exactly,
and exactly from my point of view. The gift is endless.
Now, it is in the nature of gifts, in human dealings, that

they invite a response. They do not expect a response, otherwise they would not be true gifts. They *invite* a response. And a response must come after the gift. The two edges of the gospel are not interchangeable. God's gift must come first; our response can only come second. Confirmation cannot come before baptism. I must be given the light before I can hold it up for others to see the way. Ultimately this necessity comes from the nature of the Trinity itself, as we shall see. The First Person is first because from the First Person comes love without reason, love without strings, love without any expectation of a response. Love-in-return comes from the Second Person.

The rite of confirmation as celebrated at present contains the key words of the minister to the candidate, 'Receive the seal of the gift of the Holy Spirit'. These words would seem to imply that the gift of the Holy Spirit was given already in baptism, but now the seal is placed upon the gift and it becomes more permanent. However, the gift of the Holy Spirit in baptism is permanent already, so what can these words about the seal mean? If we look at the double list I have drawn up, with 'lamb' heading the left-hand side and 'shepherd' heading the right-hand side, the meaning seems to run like this: all the titles on the right-hand side involve a divine power working through the weakness that was on the left-hand side. To be a lamb is easy: all we have to do is stay safely close to the shepherd, or if we go missing to let the shepherd find us. To be a shepherd for God, however, involves the learning of skills, endless patience, and a willingness to lay down one's life for the sheep – and the humility to ask for help or forgiveness whenever necessary. To be a little child is easy; all it needs is the sense to hold on tight to the hand of the lollipop lady when crossing the road. But then to guide another child across the road without fancying that the responsibility and the ability is mine . . . that needs divine sense. The idea of the 'coin' may help us to understand the 'seal' image, since the placing of wax upon a document, and a seal upon the wax, is a process not unlike the placing of a seal upon a coin while the metal is still molten. In baptism we are sealed with the image of a child of God. In confirmation we are sealed with the likeness of God: we are invited not simply to be children of God, but to behave in the manner of God, and as channels of God. I would really have to say that in confirmation we celebrate that we are sealed with the second gift of the Holy Spirit, which comes to us through the Second Person of the Trinity, the gift of love-in-return-for-love.

CHAPTER 11

BREAD AND WATER, THEN WINE

One idea that must strike anyone looking down my double list, corresponding to the two edges of the gospel, is that 'bread and water' and 'wine' do not seem to match up exactly with the other images on the list so far. I can picture myself as God's lamb, or as a field sown with seed, or as being guided by God ... but not as bread and water. I can see myself as called to be a shepherd and so on, but I cannot see myself as called to be wine. The first reply to this difficulty is to solve it by separating the four movements of the symphony of the gospel as follows: God loves me and provides me with bread and water; I accept his love and eat what he gives me. God then invites me to be a channel of divine love and offers me wine; I accept the wine and try to live in God's way. The 'gift of bread and water' belongs with the first movement, the first quarter of the gospel, and I accept it in the second movement. The 'gift of wine' belongs with the third movement of the gospel, and I accept it in the fourth movement.

This agrees with the way Mark's Gospel divides up the bread and water from the wine. For years I used to wonder why, if Jesus was going to create a sign of the Eucharist to come, he did the work in two halves. In the first half of the Gospel there is only bread and water. I say 'bread and water' and not just 'bread' for reasons which will soon become clearer; the immediate and obvious reason is that the sign of the feeding of the five thousand included a fulfilment of the prophecy about the sheep lying down on the green grass by the quiet waters, that is, with plenty of water to drink. It took place beside the lake; the grass was green and lush; and there were fish from the water as part of the sign. Even in the feeding of the four thousand, which took place in a desert area, still there were fish. In the later scene when they had forgotten to bring bread and they had only one loaf, the disciples were on a boat in the middle of the lake. The lake, having been such a prominent feature throughout the first half of Mark's Gospel, is never mentioned in the second half.

There is another and a very ancient reason for not forgetting the water when speaking of bread and wine. First we could recall the prayer traditionally said by the celebrant at the mixing of a little water with the wine in preparation for the Eucharist. 'By the mystery of this water and wine, may we come to share in the divinity of Christ, who humbled himself to share in our humanity.' There is a whole story behind that prayer. We can see a pattern in the writings of the early Fathers of the Church which today makes greater sense of the symbolism chosen by Jesus. Presumably those very early Christian writers were still in a better position to understand what the meaning of the symbols were in Jesus' time.

Bread was thought of as 'made by human hands', and so belonged in the same category as the human body.[1] Water was then as always a sign of life.[2] As for wine, our present-day liturgy at one point obscures the original symbolism. The prayer at the offering of the gifts at the Eucharist calls it 'fruit of the vine and work of human hands', which is the exact opposite of what St Justin and St Irenaeus called it a century after Jesus.

Justin says wine comes straight from God, and is not made by human hands; Irenaeus calls it 'heavenly', meaning 'from above', 'from heaven', not from the earth.[3] Presumably the ancient reasoning about the wine was that the fermentation of the fruit of the vine was a mystery, no human could explain it; and the resulting drink made the drinker feel divine. At all events, what we have as a result is this: bread stands for the human body; water stands for the human life or psyche; wine stands for the divine life or spirit or *pneuma*. When Jesus changes water into wine, he is proclaiming that he comes to uplift human life to a divine life. When we put a little water into the wine at the Eucharist, we are re-enacting what happened at the birth of Jesus, when divine wine was joined to our bread-and-water selves, so that our bread-and-water lives could share his divine life . . . without ceasing to be human.[4]

I said at the start of this chapter that we do not see ourselves as 'bread and water' in the same way that we might see ourselves as 'lamb of God'. I said too that we do not see ourselves as 'wine' in the same way that we might see ourselves as called to be 'shepherd'. The fact remains, the writings of the Fathers invite us to do just that. By myself and without the grace and favour of God, I am bread and water until the wine of God comes and unites with me. I, the lamb, am lost and mortal until God as Shepherd comes to pick me up. Once the wine of God has come to stay, then I can behave in a divine way without ceasing to be bread and water. Once the Shepherd has picked me up and taken me home, I can learn to become a shepherd without ceasing to be a lamb. The parallel is exact.

The shepherd by his calling may at some time be invited to give up his life or at least spend his life for his sheep. All the images on the right-hand side of my double list (shepherd; light for others; power; servant . . .) involve responsibility and cost and likely suffering. Wine as the drink for the one who willingly suffers for others implies a certain intoxication, a certain craziness to volunteer for selfless tasks. Wine in itself also suggests blood. This may only be because of Jesus' words, but the connection between wine and blood is well and truly fixed in our minds. The previous Hebrew mentality thought of 'blood' as the seat of life and the human psyche (e.g. Genesis 9:4), but Jesus shifted the emphasis on to 'water'

as the image for human life, making 'my blood' the place
of something new.

Body and Blood of Christ

We should not lose sight of the fact that the divine 'thing'
that comes to us from God through Jesus is unconditional
love. *There* is the wine. *That* is what made his blood
different from ours. The lost lamb is adopted or readopted
with no complaints, no punishments. The origin of such
love is in the Trinity, where the First Person loves the
Second Person for no reason and without asking any
return. The Second Person accepts the love and does
immediately love in return. The Second Person is the
origin of love-in-return.

Then in our history the Second Person full of the wine
received from the First Person takes on our bread and
water nature. No doubt prepared from the dawn of
history and prehistory, Jesus takes human nature from
Mary, and along with it her ancestry. There is among us
then one who knows what we need and who has what
we need.

In the Incarnation, at the first moment of Christ's
bodily existence, we can think again of the divine 'wine'
being joined to a 'bread and water' humanity. One who
so well knew God's unconditional love that he himself
was Love-in-return-for-love took on a human body and
a human life or psyche. There is in Christ then only one
person, but a person aware throughout his body and
psyche of God's unquestioning love. This love Jesus later
expresses in many ways, but more than any other in God
being his 'Abba'. The rest of us might be expected to be
able to link 'Abba' with a love that goes beyond reason
from the parent's point of view. I hope to say more in
a later chapter about why 'Abba' and not 'Mama'; but
in the present context either would be suitable, since
mothers and fathers are both capable of the love that
loves for no reason other than that 'the child is mine'.
This is the love Jesus preached, and this is the love he

urgently asked us to share and spread to all areas of human relationship.

So far, in Jesus' early life, the 'wine' is concealed within the 'water and bread' of Jesus, or in other words his divinity was not easy to see. He was full of the wine of God, but in spite of his words and actions many influential people did not recognize or want to recognize the love that is undeserved. Not only his *pneuma* was divine: as one person, all of him was divine, touched by God. So he was already the Bread that comes down from heaven, and the Water of life; but nobody could see clearly, and some did not wish ever to see. The patriots felt he had let them down by refusing to be king; the Romans were frightened of his power over the grateful crowds; the religious authorities were very much afraid of his teaching and detested it. The root of the hostility was to do with Jesus's Good News, turning upside down as it did the age-old basis of morality: from what I have called the 'doorway' morality to the 'U' form of morality.

So they killed him, or had him killed. And on the cross the wine and water were separated from the bread: the blood and water flowed from his side. His human life and his consciousness of God's love were violently separated from his body. There for all to see was love loving the undeserving, love unconditional, love forgiving its murderers. Most obvious was the blood, and its message was unmistakable. Then within three days the bread, water and wine were reunited.

When we re-enact these mysteries in the Eucharist, we say first (as Jesus taught us) 'This is my body' over the bread, the sentence meaning at that moment the whole person of Jesus, since there has been no mention of death. Then we say 'This is my blood' over the wine and water, and the death is there, because the two signs are physically separate. The body is 'here'; the blood and water is 'there', just as after the crucifixion the body was on the cross and the blood and water were on the ground. Then later a fragment of the bread is put back in the chalice, and 'bread, water and wine' are one again but

now with the wine predominant. We remember that God
has accepted the sacrifice of Jesus. Then in communion
'bread, water and wine' become one again in each of us
who eat and drink. We carry in ourselves a constant
reminder of unconditional love brought to us from God
and verified by God. God has accepted the 'U' form of
morality, so the Good News really is from God. Jesus
knew that all along, but now we too can see.

I have not included the body and blood of Christ on my
double list, outlining the two edges of the sword, because
that list concerns us, to whom and for whom Jesus came.
Each of us is only bread and water, until or unless the
true wine of unconditional love comes and mingles with
us. Then already we are divine, even if (as with the Good
Thief) the divinity is hidden. The Good Thief can hardly
be said to have given up his life for Jesus – it was
the other way round! But given time, anyone who has
been touched by that hidden wine will let it be seen, in
unselfish actions, just as surely as the hidden seed from
God will come to light in God's good time.

There is in the New Testament more than one hint
that Jesus' blood has to do with his ancestry in a rather
pro-masculine fashion. God is his Father, Mary is his
mother, we are his brothers and sisters, and that is
why God is our Father and Mary is our mother. The
implication seems at times to be, that Jesus got his body
from Mary, but his blood from God. Therefore as Son of
God in this manner, heaven is his inheritance because the
first-born son inherits the greater share of the father's
fortune; and Jesus shares his inheritance with the rest of
us if we are willing to be children of God in his way. Now
I do not believe in the sort of biology of ancient times that
appears to have thought that life and blood came from
the father's seed, but the solid body from the mother.
Nor do I think there is any reason to believe that Jesus
was tied to such a biology. What he meant by calling God
'Abba' and insisting on it has, I believe, nothing to do
with masculine prejudice, as I hope to argue later on. For
the moment, we may simply insist that the blood of Jesus

shed on the cross was no more divine, no more 'precious'
and imperishable than the water he shed or the body
they were shed from. They were all equally precious, all
equally worth infinitely more than the price paid for them
to Judas. In human terms they all three perished in being
separated each from the other, though they did not stay
dead so long as to 'see corruption', in fulfilment of the
prophetic psalm. What never perished was the person of
Jesus, loved unconditionally by God and loving-in-return
unconditionally. In the Resurrection the body and the
human psyche no longer hide the divinity, which shines
through. The bread is seen to be our bread from heaven;
the water is a stream of living water that murmurs within
us 'Come to the Father';[5] the wine and the blood are
visible and everlasting reminders of the kind of love God
has for us. We simply cannot break his love.

St Paul prays a blessing on the 'spirit and soul and
body' of each of the Christians in Thessalonika. One who
has welcomed the unconditional love of God and begun to
share it with others has a 'spirit and soul and body' just
as Jesus did. We have a different kind of body and life
now, and Jesus was the first to have such. And Mary was
and is where such a body and life came into the world.

There are two more aspects of this mystery of body
and blood I wish to touch on finally: the 'two-edged
sword' and the notion of 'flesh'. First, 'the word of God
is living and active, sharper than any two-edged sword,
piercing to the division of soul and spirit, of joints and
marrow . . .' (Hebrews 4:12). If we imagine before us on
a table, bread, water and wine, the word of God, working
in the mysteries we have been considering, cuts a clear
line between the water and wine, the soul (psyche) and
spirit, in announcing that the two only came together in
the Incarnation and only come together in us through
the Good News. The word about the death of Jesus also
cuts a clear line between the water and the bread, the
human life of Jesus and his body, in that the life left
his body for our sakes. We could say, the marrow was
separated from the joints, the bones . . . the life left his

bones. We are talking about three realities, the bread, the water, the wine; there are two spaces between them, clearly demarcated as a result of the Word of God.

About the notion of 'flesh', my main point would be to aver that 'flesh' usually means much the same as 'bread and water', or humanity, but humanity *as subject to temptation*, whereas 'bread and water' or body and psyche means simply human weakness, without moral overtones. Thus, 'and the Word became flesh' (John 1:14) would mean that the one carrying the Word of God – the Word that says ever 'You are my beloved . . .' – became human and subject to temptation. When Paul says that 'to set the mind on the flesh is death' (Romans 8:6), he means that to go along with the temptations of the flesh brings death. Jesus on the other hand says, 'the bread that I shall give for the life of the world is my flesh' (John 6:51) because Jesus being one with the Spirit knows well the ways to overcome the basic temptations.

The basic temptations to which the flesh is prone are, first, to decide that God is like 'a severe man; you take up what you did not lay down, and reap what you did not sow'. Secondly, and in consequence, to decide not to trust God. These two temptations, if yielded to, cancel out the first two movements of the symphony which is the Good News. The third temptation is then to try and earn heaven, either out of fear of God or out of sheer pride. The fourth temptation is to despair when this does not succeed: either that or to turn to hypocrisy. In God's mercy the absolute failure can lead to humility instead of despair, or to humility following despair, and then God can try again with the Good News. Such was the pattern of the Old Testament, leading finally to an understanding of the depths of God's mercy shown to us in Christ. The third and fourth temptations are in effect a return to the Old Testament, this time cancelling out the third and fourth movements of the 'symphony'. The Way of Jesus takes the flesh and conquers temptation.

In summary, then, the four movements. First, I am simply bread-and-water. There were even those among the early Christians who celebrated the Eucharist with only bread and water, because they felt themselves to be too unworthy of the divinity.[6] Second, the wine of God penetrates me and I become a divine child, a found lamb, a child with my hand in a powerful hand. Third, I am invited to share this wine, this unquestioning love, with others in gratitude to the One who gave it to me. Fourth, I let the wine flow from me.

CHAPTER 12

FREE; COSTLY

A lamb does not have to pay for its existence: that comes free. A lost lamb does not have to pay for being sought, cherished, picked up and taken home. The shepherd however may have to pay to possess the lamb in the first place, and he may have to pay dear to rescue a lost lamb or one threatened by wild beasts. The first two movements of the 'symphony' of the Good News cost us nothing. We do not have to pay for our existence, and we do not have to pay for being chosen and adopted by God as his own. Christ had to pay dearly to redeem us, each and every one, because he was the Shepherd and he laid down his life for us. Likewise if we volunteer to become one of his disciples and let the wine of his love flow through us, the price may well be high. The third and fourth movements of the symphony are usually costly, but they are precious and desirable none the less, since they imitate God's own behaviour.

This same pattern runs through all the images on my double list: the images on the left-hand side are free; those on the right are costly. A dark mass like the moon does not pay for its own existence, nor does it have to pay for the light of the sun that makes it the queen of the night. I do not have to pay for the light lit from the paschal candle which warms my face and warms my heart with the knowledge that I am God's child. But to hold up the light and share it with others, that can often be costly. A child being escorted across a dangerous road usually has no fear; trust comes naturally, and costs nothing. But the parent or teacher or lollipop lady bears the anxiety, and takes the responsibility for seeing the child safely across. A son or a daughter does not have to pay for being son or daughter. Existence comes to us freely, and usually parents love their children and do not expect payment for parenting, at least as long as the child is little. Jesus noted to Peter one time that the kings of the earth do not take toll or tribute from their children: 'The children are free' (Matthew 17:26 NRSV). In a similar fashion the house or stone placed upon a rock foundation does not have to worry about how strong it is in itself. The strain is carried by the foundation.

A fish does not have to make an effort to be caught! A lost coin simply has to be lying there, the object of someone else's wish. A field does not have to plough or sow itself. Travellers very badly wounded can only wait for the emergency services. It costs nothing to be waited on by God, with gifts of nature or grace, or personal gifts. Martha reckoned that Mary was getting something for nothing, as Mary sat there at Jesus' feet. Baptism and repentance cost nothing, since it is far easier to turn and face a loving God than to run away from a God we believe to be a hard taskmaster. Our bread-and-water lives cost us nothing; the added gift of wine to raise us to the divine is also pure gift. Forgiveness is free; we do not have to earn forgiveness, in the beginning of our conversion or ever. To be loved is free, to have the Spirit come to us is free, and even the gift of trust or faith to believe in God's love comes free. All that is necessary is free.

The costly things are all on the other edge of the sword, on the right-hand side of the double list. To shed light, to feel power go out from ourselves, to support others in their weakness, to spend long weary nights fishing . . . these are the images of the costly side of life with God. Coin-seekers are patient and painstaking, sowers must plough before they sow, must sow, must wait, and only then will they reap. Guides must be careful of enemies and of pitfalls, for themselves and for their charges. Servants and slaves work hard to save their masters and mistresses trouble. Martha had all the serving to

attend to, while Mary just sat there. Jesus' mission grew
out of his being God's Son, but what a costly response
was invited by that precious gift. The wine is a gift,
but then we are invited to pour it out for others. To be
forgiven is easy, but to forgive others is not. To follow
the promptings of the Spirit and love others as we have
been loved ourselves, that is costly. In God's unfailing
courtesy, all these costly gifts-in-return are voluntary.
God still loves us even if we fail to make a generous
response.

God gives us all the gifts pictured on the left-hand side
of the list, invites us to the glory of living in his way as
on the right-hand side of the list, then forgives us each
and every time we fail. There is no comparison between
the size of God's gift to us, and our gift in return. I
once compared the disparity to this: some kind person
gives me a million pounds, and in return I send a card
simply saying 'Thank you'. The comparison Jesus made
was between a generous person letting another off a debt
of ten thousand talents, who then was simply expected to
cancel a debt of one hundred denarii. We are asked to
forgive others their sins against us, simply that, a mere
speck compared with all we owe to God, if he should
decide to call in the debt.

Jesus objected to the way the temple at Jerusalem was
run. The wealthy and the healthy were favoured, at the
expense of the poor and the sick. The temple authorities
were, in his view, facing the wrong way, with their backs
to the light. They were in fact following the 'doorway'
style of morality instead of taking to themselves the 'U'
style which Jesus was proclaiming. They were making
people pay for God's greater favour, payment either in
cash or by way of strict adherence to the Law, whereas
God's love is free. They were diverting money into their
own coffers instead of giving the fruit of the temple back
to God. They started with worldly money, and tried to
win even more money back from God, instead of starting
with God's currency and giving the fruit back to God. All
their beautiful buildings and their precious stones would

come to nothing because they were not founded on the imperishable, unbreakable love of God for each of his children. They were based on human effort, on fortune, and failing those, on appearances.

The fig tree that withered was a symbol of the temple and its inadequacy to the task. The tree looked beautiful, but was unable to produce fruit at all seasons. Only the tree whose seed comes from God could do that. All others are weeds and thorns and thistles, sown by darkness, unable to be useful, and therefore bound to perish. Jesus offers the truly precious wine of God's unconditional love to each and every one, creating a new temple in every heart. The old temple started from the ground, tried and failed to reach heaven, then returned to the earth from which it came. Jesus' new temple comes down from heaven, picks up poor humanity, and returns to heaven in gratitude. The gift is free, we do not have to pay for it; the gratitude can be expensive, but because it is a response to such a gift, the expense can be discounted by the grateful one.

Detachment

What about the pearl of great value, what about the treasure in the field, to which Jesus compared the kingdom of heaven? Did not Jesus say, whoever found them would have to sell everything in order to buy the field, or the pearl (Matthew 13:44–46)? Does not that make the kingdom very expensive, whereas I am saying salvation is free? Yes, and no. Jesus does not describe the speculator or the merchant as making a loss, but as making a profit, which means that the field and the pearl in fact cost nothing in the end. Similarly when Jesus says, 'Those who want to save their life will lose it, and those who lose their life for my sake, and for the sake of the gospel, will save it', he is not speaking about the cost of being a disciple, but of the cost of the initial acceptance of God's unconditional love. He is speaking about something necessary, whereas going on to be a disciple is optional.

In order to become God's lamb, one must abandon total independence and let oneself be taken home. In order to find the power of God, one must become a little child. Those who want to shine with divine light must acknowledge their own darkness. To become God's son or daughter means relegating our own parents to second place in our lives. The fish must let itself be caught, and trust God for the future. And so on, down the list.

Earthly values must also be relegated to second place: the fig tree will wither, but the tree of life is eternal; the temple will be destroyed by enemies or by time, no matter how fine and precious its stones seem now. Money will perish, jewels and gold will perish in time, but the precious unquestioning love of God will last for ever, and we with it if we only trust. Jesus, and the disciple of Jesus, work in the opposite direction to the 'temptations of human nature' described in the previous chapter. Where someone in the fourth temptation is in despair over worldly failure, Jesus gives hope; where someone has turned to hypocrisy, Jesus faces them with the truth. Where someone in the third temptation is all for human success and glory, Jesus inclines them to poverty and simplicity of life. Where someone in the second or first temptations has a wrong picture of God and cannot find trust, Jesus shows the true picture, and with it the ability to trust and to let oneself be led and loved.

To become a lamb, then, costs nothing in real terms, but it does mean abandoning or 'selling' the myth of total human independence first. Becoming a shepherd on the other hand (whilst remaining a lamb) is costly in real terms, but in the light of love the cost does not cut us as deeply as it would without the call of Jesus. Love takes away some of the pain, some of the sting. Once we, as shepherds, are assured that the responsibility for success rests with the Chief Shepherd and with the owner of the flock, then we can accept that this is a labour of love, with a beginning, a middle, and a happy end. A little child at a road crossing can be quite happy linking with another child, so long as the other hand is guided by an adult.

There is a similar blessing of peace that comes to the
one who is detached from, unattached to, the need to
make a success in human terms. William Blake in a
short poem, observed that if we try to possess a joy,
we lose it, whereas if we 'kiss it as it flies', we live in
eternity's sunrise. Pick a wild flower and it dies; leave it
be, and it lasts for weeks. Children playing a board game
such as Ludo often fall to arguing: three of them because
they are losing, and the fourth because the others will not
carry on playing once they see they are losing. It takes the
wisdom of years to notice that the game is much more fun
if we cease from being intent simply on our own corner.
There are four players and four plays to enjoy, not just
one. All the world is mine, so long as I do not lay exclusive
claim on any one section of it. 'Blessed are the meek, for
they shall inherit the earth.' Jesus' contemporaries made
a scapegoat out of him, took the earth for themselves,
pushing Jesus off it altogether: but the world and all
within it was and is his. One who possesses the wine
from God need worry no longer about things that have
a mortal span of life, since the divine version of all is
possessed already.

The divine and everlasting temple is already there in
the heart of anyone who lets God in. The tree of life is
there for anyone who remembers the cross of Jesus and
relies upon it. The fruit of the tree of life is there at
every season in the body and blood of Jesus, in Paradise
regained. Already there is a new heaven and a new earth
for anyone who accepts the forgiveness of God and tries
to forgive others.

CHAPTER 13

FORGIVEN; FORGIVING

One of the titles of God is 'Forgiveness'. God is Love, and God is Forgiveness. Where forgiveness is, God is; where forgiveness is not, God is not. As far as God is concerned, our sins are forgiven from all eternity, before we were conceived, before we were born, when we were born, when we were children, before we committed sins, while we committed sins, since then, now and into eternity. Those among Christians who celebrate reconciliation as a sacrament do so not in order to have their sins forgiven, but to celebrate the fact that their sins are already forgiven.

When, in the Apostles' Creed, I say, 'I believe in the forgiveness of sins', I cannot be allowed to mean simply, 'I believe in the forgiveness of my sins', without meaning 'I believe in the forgiveness of everyone else's sins as well'. Jesus' parables and teachings make it clear that if I decide to believe in a world where 'pay up' is the watchword, then that is the world I will have to put up with. If I make retribution my god, then retribution is what I will get. Such is the nature of reality: reality is forgiveness, and if I fly in the face of reality, then I will end up with a distortion. There is nothing half-hearted about forgiveness: either all debts are cancelled, or all debts are to be collected. If I make a substitute god out of 'the payment of debts', then that god will send the bailiffs round to my door. Not the real God, whose name is Forgiveness. Those who follow the 'doorway' form of morality, and who therefore are facing away from God and forgiveness,

tend to be judgmental. Success and merit are the things
that matter, and wealth and health, so that immediately
there are comparisons. Anyone doing better than me is a
threat, anyone cheating me is a menace. Anyone I do not
like is seen as getting in my way, anyone actually hurting
me is seen as preventing my growth. Thorns and thistles
are what Jesus compared these unforgiving attitudes to,
weeds that choke other plants without doing any real
good themselves. If, moreover, I am doing badly, I tend
to judge and despise myself as well as everyone else. Even
God seems to be against me, since my back is turned on
God and all I can see is darkness. Jesus in his teaching
appealed to any who would listen, to learn to forgive their
enemies, and to pray for those who hurt them.

The breakthrough would not come from nowhere;
first would come, as a gift from God, an awareness of
sinfulness, and a desire to be forgiven. Then there would
be a readiness to listen to Jesus saying, 'Judge not, and
you will not be judged' (Luke 6:37), and so a willingness
to try and forgive. Such at any rate was the path I found
in my own life: from pride, to an awareness of fragility
and the possibility of failing, and then a real effort not
to judge others, from which came at last a knowledge of
how total is God's forgiveness. Nowadays when I forgive,
it is not so much out of a desire to avoid judgment, as from
a desire to thank the God of forgiveness and to be like
him in my turn. Though I must admit, the freedom from
judgment is something so precious that I would forgive
anyone anything to preserve it. I still maintain that being
forgiven is free, but forgiving others is costly; and what
is free is necessary, whereas what is costly is voluntary.
Let me explain how this could apply to forgiveness. We
are forgiven, that is absolute. We cannot, we do not have
to, earn forgiveness: the moment we want it, we have it.
Those who do not forgive others have blinded themselves,
and as long as they do not forgive, they will never see
that they are forgiven. Hence Jesus' warnings, as when
he says that if we do not forgive others, our heavenly
Father will not forgive us either (see Matthew 6:15).

Will not *be able to* forgive, is what it comes to, since the unforgivingness blocks out the real God. Once the gift of God breaks through to an unforgiving person who hears Jesus, and that person becomes aware of the need for forgiveness, then there comes a readiness to try forgiving others. Then in time comes a deeper awareness of how forgiving the real God is. From then on, the effort to forgive others is taken up voluntarily, though hardly ever with complete success. But just as a not very successful shepherd is forgiven by God and encouraged to start again, so also anyone who finds forgiving difficult can be forgiven and encouraged to start ever afresh.

This process shows the importance of John the Baptist, in that he prepared the way for Jesus by getting people to acknowledge their sinfulness and their need of forgiveness. Those who really listened to John were ready for Jesus telling them to forgive others. Those who would not listen to John were those who would not listen to Jesus, because they were satisfied with themselves and they objected to Jesus' leniency with sinners. We do not earn forgiveness by forgiving others: we simply take the log out of our own eye so as to be able to see we are already freely forgiven. The situation is like that of the monkey who puts his paw between narrow bars and clutches a tasty fruit. He cannot get his paw back without letting go of the fruit. At any time he could let go, but the story has it he clings on to the fruit until the hunter catches him. So for an unforgiving person who has no intention of ever forgiving: Jesus spells out the danger that such a one might never see forgiveness. To my mind this ultimately is the sin that 'will not be forgiven' (Matthew 12:31–32), since it means shutting out the Holy Spirit by which we call God 'Abba', and choosing a taskmaster god, an unforgiving god, instead.

We can see the way the gift of God works in the case of the Good Thief, crucified beside Jesus. He acknowledged that he was a sinner; he used Jesus as a mediator to ask for forgiveness for himself. He did not earn forgiveness. But it is noticeable that he refrained from judging Jesus, and he upbraided his fellow thief for doing just that.

The story of the Prodigal Son (prodigal with his inheritance) and the elder brother is endlessly illuminating. Jesus told the story for the benefit of the Pharisees and the scribes (Luke 15:1–2, 11–32), so really the elder brother is the one for us to identify with first of all, since he was the 'pharisee'. How many good, law-abiding, honest people puzzle over that story, and find themselves sympathizing with the elder brother. Whereas Jesus is saying in effect that when the glorious moment comes of entering into Paradise, the first person I will see, basking in God's love and forgiveness, will be the very person I could never stand! And behind that person, all the very classes of people I have found most difficult in life. We are not told whether the elder brother went in to the celebrations, because the answer lies with the hearer or reader of the parable. If I am willing to share heaven with other sinners, heaven is mine already; if I am not, then I am in danger of shutting myself out. God does not shut me out.

The other side of the coin is the glorious freedom that comes of admitting my own fragility, asking for forgiveness, letting God forgive me and letting God forgive everybody else as well. I live then in a forgiven world, with no sword of judgment hanging over it, and such a world is worth giving up the other for, infinitely so. A story that helped me very much early on in my life concerned and old monk who broke all the rules of the abbey throughout his life. When he was on his deathbed, the Father Abbot was puzzled that the old man looked so serene, even cheerful. 'Do you not worry, Brother, that you are soon to be judged, and that you have lived a very poor sort of a life?' The old man replied that he had had a vision from Jesus, who told him, 'Well now, Brother, you have broken every rule in the book except one. Which one? "Judge not, and you will not be judged". You chose well. I will keep my promise, and you need not fear the judgment'. Whereupon the old monk died, with a smile on his face. It may have been the back door into heaven, but it was good enough for me!

I have mentioned already the parable of the unforgiving debtor, who was let off a debt of ten thousand talents but would not let off someone who owed him a debt roughly ten thousand times less (Matthew 18:23–35). We owe God for our lives, our world, our friends and relations, our food, all that we enjoy; we owe for our forgiveness over each and every sin and failing, and for the divine 'wine' that transforms us; we owe for all the gifts particular to ourselves, the special way we are and look and feel and the special things we do well. None of these could we repay if we lived in a world where 'pay up' was god. By comparison, the things anyone else owes us are insignificant, a mere speck in the eye.

One of the things I learnt with gratitude during lectures on theology was that the 'character' of baptism lies in this, that it gives me a permanent place at the table. The 'character' of certain sacraments refers to the fact that those sacraments are given once and for all and do not need repeating – cannot be repeated, in fact. When I am adopted by God I am given a permanent place at his table, with my name on it. If I am slow in coming to God, and others say to him, 'Shall we shift his place and all move up one?', God will not allow this. Similarly, if and when I reach my Father's house, with forgiveness in my heart for all whom I find there, and someone else would have me excluded because of the harm I did him or her, God will say, 'His place is fixed: forgive him, and stay with us, please'.

The Lord's Prayer as given in the Gospels themselves includes the words, 'And forgive us our debts, as we also have forgiven our debtors' (Matthew 6:10) or, 'and forgive us our sins, for we ourselves forgive every one who is indebted to us' (Luke 11:4). Particularly in Matthew's version, and also in the liturgical version said by Christians everywhere, this part of the prayer reads like a boomerang: we loose off a prayer, and it comes back to us. If we are unwary and return to being

unforgiving in the meantime, the prayer could turn out
to be a prayer against ourselves instead of for ourselves.
We cannot always alter our feelings towards an enemy:
in that case the best solution is to pray for the enemy,
as Jesus said. I can surely always pray for my enemy
to be converted, to become gentle, to have a change of
heart, to cease from ever again doing to anyone what was
done to me. The New Testament does not expect me to
become 'best friends' with anyone who has behaved in
a nasty way towards me: even St Paul advised Timothy
to be wary of Alexander the coppersmith, who had done
him great harm.

The boomerang works in this life, not just in some
future life. If I am very strict about rules and regulations,
then I have to keep them myself. If I explode into anger
at the sight of litter on the ground, then I condemn
myself to picking up bits of paper, or at least worrying
myself sick about them, for the rest of my life, or until
I learn to forgive the litter-droppers. If punctuality is
an essential for me, and I come down heavily on all
who are late for things, then the moment I look like
being late for something myself, I become distressed out
of all proportion. Either that, or I become a hypocrite with
double standards: one rule for everyone else and another
rule for me.

We can see in our ordinary lives how unforgivingness
rebounds on the unforgiving one, since that is the nature
of reality. Those who make law and order the ultimate
god make themselves responsible for everyone else's
behaviour, which is an impossible burden. And how
quickly we ourselves do what we have just condemned
in another. How much better to climb down from the
judge's chair, take off our gown and wig, and acquit
everyone else there is. We need to forgive the saints,
for being so good and so impossible to live up to; we
need to forgive the sinner as Jesus did, whatever the
sin. If we look carefully at the Gospels, we find that Jesus
never condemned any sinner, only the self-righteous who
condemned others and who denied that they themselves

were sinners at all! He condemned many sins, but no sinners. The only time he gave physical expression to anger was over the buying and selling in the temple, where people were putting God's love up to the highest bidders. God's love and forgiveness is free.

Judges, magistrates, teachers and parents and others in authority would do well to follow the example of Jesus. They have to have their standards, and know the kind of behaviour they think right, and to do their best to see that those in their charge conform. But when things go wrong, they should always remember to separate the sin from the sinner, condemning the one and yet forgiving, not judging, the other. God has given no one authority to call another person a villain; in fact Jesus gives the distinct impression that whatever name we call another, that name belongs to us and not to the other (see Matthew 5:21–26). It seems that only a fool would call anyone else a fool, after hearing Jesus' Sermon on the Mount!

At a very basic level, we do not 'win friends and influence people' by criticizing them at the outset. The only people Jesus criticized were the critics, the 'scribes and Pharisees' of his world. When Jesus was invited to speak in the synagogue, he sat down to do so, putting himself on a level with his audience. We are told by Jesus to love others as we love ourselves, and so we need to treat ourselves as the sinners we are and be forgiving with ourselves as well as with others. Children flourish best under a teacher who encourages and does not condemn. Likewise we get the best out of ourselves by not thinking we have to be saying 'Sorry' to ourselves all the time.

In summary, then. In the New Covenant our sins are forgiven, freely. But we have to accept forgiveness, and for that we have to see the need. If we are unforgiving with others we blind ourselves to the need for our own forgiveness. So the two things go together: the need to forgive and the realization that we ourselves need forgiving. Jesus therefore insists that we forgive others. When we have seen our need and started to forgive

others, we then realize more and more that God loves
and forgives us freely. The need to forgive others then
seems more like an invitation, to be more like God. It is an
invitation rather than a command, at least in the sense
that Jesus sees we cannot yet forgive once and for all, but
need to forgive again and again, seventy-seven times in
the day perhaps, because our hearts do not always follow
our heads. As with the command to love (it is the same
command really), we will never reach perfection in our
mortal lives.

We forgive others not in order to be forgiven, but in
order to *see* that we are already forgiven. Forgiving is
not so much something we do, as a way of letting the real
God work through us. To judge others is to play at being
God, and a false god at that; the sooner we can detach
ourselves from such a habit the better. In essence, the
four movements of the symphony of the gospel in terms
of forgiveness are: first, God is forgiving; second, I believe
in the forgiveness of sins; third, God invites me to forgive
all others as I have been forgiven; fourthly, I try and try
again to do so.

CHAPTER 14

'YOU ARE MY BELOVED';
'THIS IS MY BELOVED'

I have already suggested how the Good News from heaven to Jesus falls into two halves and four movements. God says to Jesus, 'You are my beloved Son'; Jesus accepts the word. God invites Jesus to witness to the world what it means to be a child of God; Jesus accepts and carries out God's will. Moreover, the Good News as it is brought to fruition in the rest of us in the human race follows the same pattern.

What I wish to do in this chapter and the next is to match up the Church's teaching about the Trinity with the images on the two-sided list I have been working from. My premise is that the First Person of the Trinity is the One who loved without first having been loved; the Second Person of the Trinity is the one who is Love-in-return-for-love; the Third Person is the personal Relationship between them. How does this fit in with the images on the double list?

The example that has always struck me most forcibly is that of the rock. The rock does not come first on my list, but for the sake of vividness I start there. When we listen to Jesus, and act on his words, then our house is built on a rock. Jesus is my Rock. Jesus in his earthly life prayed the psalms, and was accustomed to call God his Rock. Jesus is built on the Rock of God, and we are built on the Rock of Jesus. Yet the Rock of God is not built on anything – anything or anyone. I find the image overwhelming: a Rock, completely solid as no other rock, yet built on no other. Not floating in space, but deeply founded, without being founded on anyone or anything else.

This brings to mind expressions from theology, about the uncaused cause, the first link in the eternal chain, the first in the line of analogy. More personally, God alone can say, 'I am who I am', as he said to Moses from the burning bush, after which there is nothing more to be asked. God is not anyone's son or daughter, does not need to be defined in relation to anyone else as a source of God. And all the time this is saying the same thing as 'God the First Person is the One who loves without having been first loved by anyone else'. The First Person is first in the chain of love. Nobody taught God to love: God *is* Love, Love everlasting, Love unshakable, Love unbreakable, the Love on whom all other love is founded.

God is not just the Shepherd; God is the owner of the whole flock. God is the first source of the light which is love. All other lights, even those of Christ and the Holy Spirit, are from the one source which itself has no source. God is the source of all power: the kingdom is his, and will be handed back to him by Christ. God has no father, no mother. In gospel pictures, God is the owner of the fishing boat, not just an ordinary fisher; his is the treasury and the treasure, he is no ordinary coin-gatherer. The field is his, and the crop of wheat; the vineyard is his, and the wine that comes from it. He is the end of the Way, he is the exemplar of all service whilst all honour is due to him. He alone has the right to forgive, but is everlasting forgiveness.

Christ is the true mirror of the Light of God. It is worth reflecting upon the attempts of the ancient philosophers to understand God. The Greek thinkers, such as Plato, came to understand that there is beauty here and beauty there, yet no beautiful person or thing or situation is Beauty itself. The beauty we see must be simply a reflection of the real Beauty which has its own existence. So too with Justice, Goodness, Truth and all virtues. They saw, moreover, that ultimately all these sublime ideas must be One, must exist in a

Being who was the One from whom all the virtues we see are derived.[1] What Plato and the others did not recognize was that many virtues need another person for their very existence. If there is gratitude here, gratitude there, yet no grateful person is Gratitude itself, then there must be in God Gratitude as well. And Praise, and Admiration, and Thanks, and Faithfulness, and Love-in-return-for-love. A one-personal God cannot really be the source of all these, singly. Christ is that necessary Second Person of God, made flesh for us; Christ is the Reflection of God. And between Love-with-no-conditions and Love-in-return-for-love is the Relationship we know as the Holy Spirit, the Third Person.

Because Jesus is the Image, the Reflection of the Light, he is in that sense not as great as the Light: 'The Father is greater than I' (John 10:29; 14:28). Yet we can safely say, now that it has been revealed to us, that there must be at least two Persons in God, since Love has to love Someone. Moreover, to have two Persons at a distance but unrelated is not love either. Relationships exist in our world, and they must have their source in God. Just as the reflecting virtues such as gratitude have their source in the Second Person, so two-way relationships have their source in the Third Person.

Christian teaching has always been that God did not *have* to create, that creation was and is a free act of God. So the first exemplar of love and love-returned must have been direct from God and back to God, and not depending on anyone else as the receiver of love. When we humans love God back, we show our love for God by loving others; in the Trinity, apart from or before creation, the Second Person must love the First, in return for love, and there the story ends. The Light shines on the Second Person, the Second Person reflects the Light back to the First Person, who is well pleased.

In God, the First Person is the Shepherd, the Second Person is the Lamb of God, and freely so. The Second Person is not only the cherished Lamb, the Second Person loves in return, so is in some sense 'Shepherd' to the

First Person, filling the unspoken desire to be loved in return. We may surely see the father of the Prodigal Son as being in some sense fulfilled by the return of the lost son. This two-way exclusive love is most clearly seen in our world in a happy marriage, where each is shepherd to the other's lamb, quite apart from any children there may be to the marriage. Where even the most perfect marriage differs from the love in the Trinity is that a marriage is based on reflected love, from both sides of the relationship. Neither partner is able to 'love without having first been loved'. Both have been created by a God who loved them.

We can know very little about love within the Trinity except in so far as that love comes into our created world and is spoken about by Jesus. As we have seen, the First Person loves without having first been loved, and does so freely. The Second Person accepts that love, freely. The Second Person gives back love, again with no conditions, again freely. The First Person accepts and cherishes that love, freely. The Spirit or Relationship between the two goes in two directions: first from Father to Son, then back from Son to Father. We can imagine the First Person saying to the Second in all eternity: 'You are my Beloved'. But can we imagine the First Person saying, even if there were no creation, 'This is my Beloved'? Possibly, the First Person might say this about the Second, to the Spirit, the Third Person, in accepting the returned love as a true reflection of the love that was first given (compare John 7:18; 15:26).

At the transfiguration, Jesus shared the vision with Peter, James and John. There it was the Father's voice from heaven which witnessed to Jesus from the cloud, 'This is my beloved Son; listen to him'. From then on it became clearer and clearer that Jesus would have to suffer in order to fulfil the Father's will. The way in which Jesus most clearly reflects the kind of love the First Person of the Trinity has for us is seen in his love for the people who hated him. Not even Jesus could demonstrate at first hand 'love without ever having been first loved by another'; but what he does demonstrate is love with absolutely no experience of love coming back to him from those he loved. This is the kind of love he tells his disciples to look for, and to be delighted if they find it in their hearts to give to others. For example, when we have a party, to invite those who cannot pay us back by inviting us to a party. To pray for enemies, and do good to those who hate us. Not to be dismayed at rejection or persecution, but rather to rejoice at such trouble, because then we are most clearly behaving like the First Person of the Trinity, like Love itself.

How, we might wonder, could the Second Person of the Trinity give such love within the Trinity itself, without a rejecting world through which to demonstrate the love of enemies? There are hints in the story of the Prodigal Son. In the first place, the father of the young man lets him go, even though it probably breaks his heart to do so. Love with no conditions is painful. The father is willing to wait and hope. Jesus the storyteller is telling us that love with no conditions is the only sure way of receiving love in return. The son comes back, and he in his turn makes no conditions. He does not expect to be loved again; he is willing to be a servant and work to earn some love. He too is taking a risk. Perhaps his father will not have him back on any terms. The risk pays off, and that is the way of love. The First Person loves the Second, with no guarantee of a return. The Second Person loves in return, but freely *and* without any guarantee that the First Person will accept the love-in-return. There is risk on both sides, but the trust is justified.

The story of Jesus' work, and rejection and death while praying for his enemies, and his resurrection and ascension to heaven where Love came from, tells us over and over that God's love for us has no conditions attached. Whatever state we find ourselves in, we will be welcome at home.

CHAPTER 15

THE SPIRIT LOVES;
THE SPIRIT CALLS

In my room I have hanging down below one of the bookshelves two small white pottery doves. They were sent to me by friends from El Salvador at the time of the civil war there in the 1980s. They are called 'peace doves'. They swing around a lot in the least draught or breeze, but I try to have them facing, one towards me and the other as if flying away from me. Between them they then remind me of the Holy Spirit. The one coming towards me reminds me of the way the Spirit comes gently in baptism and from then on like the warming light of the baptismal candle. You can see the eyes of the dove and they are peaceful and friendly. The other dove, flying away, reminds me of the same Spirit's subsequent invitation to go out to others, to hold up my light for everyone in the house to see by. The pottery dove flying away does not show its eyes, so the attitude is less warm, like that of someone calling 'Come, follow me'.

The same two attitudes of the Spirit, the attitude of gift-bearer and the attitude of one who calls, apply to each of the pairs on my double list. The Spirit comes to me making me God's lamb, goes away from me inviting me to be a shepherd for God. Coming, the Spirit brings to this child the strength of an adult to look after me; going, the invitation is to take the hand of another child while still holding on to the adult. The dove coming towards me assures me I am God's child; going on its way it invites me to be God's servant. The Spirit comes bringing God's rock-like love; going, asks me to carry others as I am carried. The dove that looks at me tells me I am the fish caught in God's net, or the coin cherished and finally found; the dove whose eyes I cannot see invites me to follow and become an apostle, a fisher of people, a collector of the 'coins' with God's image on them. The Spirit coming brings the seed, the word of God, and waters my dry ground; the Spirit moving on calls me to grow a good crop.

The dove that comes shows the way; the dove that goes says, 'Now you know the way, show it to others'. The gentler attitude of the dove shows God waiting upon me; the more valiant attitude shows how I can wait upon God. The dove coming says to sit with Mary; the dove going says to work like Martha. The Spirit coming says I am God's beloved child; the Spirit moving on says everyone is to listen to me, which means I am to speak up for being God's child. The Spirit comes to me as wine comes to bread-and-water, giving me a totally new, totally unique relationship with God. 'God shows no partiality' (Acts 10:34; Romans 2:11), God has no favourites, so that each of us is as precious to God as anyone else; once we realize that, then the call comes to tell others they are equally precious to God, to let the wine flow through us to others. The gift of the dove is free; the call of the dove is costly. The gift we must receive; the call we simply do our best with, and if the best is very poor we look again at the gift, the gift of forgiveness. The dove coming towards me brings forgiveness; the dove flying away calls me to forgive others as I have been forgiven myself.

'Do not be astonished that I said to you, "You must be born from above." The wind blows where it chooses, and you hear the sound of it, but you do not know where it comes from or where it goes. So it is with everyone who is born of the Spirit' (John 3:7–8 NRSV). The wind of the Spirit blows from the Father, and then the wind goes back to the Father, having altered me in its coming and its going. The Spirit proceeds from the Father and from the Son. The Spirit proceeds from the Father to the Son and then goes back again from the Son to the Father. The

wind blows firstly from God to me, to Christ in me, to the
adopted child of God that is me. In the other metaphor,
the wine coming to my bread-and-water transforms me
and draws me into the life of the Trinity. By the power
of the Father I become son or daughter; by the power
of the Son I am, in return, able to love others without
expecting any return from them.   The great divide in
the Catholic Church between East and West was over
the question of whether the Holy Spirit proceeds from
the Father alone, or from the Son as well. Clearly, I
have been siding with the Western view. Love-in-return
is fundamentally different from first-love, even though
the one is inspired by the other. Love-in-return cannot,
of its very nature, come first from the First Person, but
must come in the first instance from a second Person.
Also, the Second Person was totally free to love back or
not to love back, so the love of the Second Person was not
an automatic reaction caused totally by the First Person.
In our own life of grace we need first the First Person to
love us; then, the Second Person to accept the love. Then,
we need the Second Person to call or invite us to love
valiantly in return; then, we need the First Person to
accept our love-in-return. Thus in all of this, the Trinity
is at work, and one could say that we ourselves do little
else but give permission for it to happen – though in the
daily struggle it feels a lot more personal and distressing
than the mere giving of permission.

I am 'spirit and soul and body' (1 Thessalonians
5:23), that is to say in eucharistic metaphor 'wine and
water and bread'. The wine comes to me as a gift, my
personal one-to-one relationship with God, not just with
the Father but with the Son as well. The Son becomes my
brother. The two-way Relationship between the First and
Second Persons becomes a gift to me, the gift of the Spirit.
The only reason the spirit in me does not have a capital
'S' is to show the difference between an adopted child
and the 'only begotten', though I do believe each of us
is as precious to God as God's own Son, since God has no
favourites, and was willing to give up his only Son to save

the rest of us (cf Romans 8:32; 1 John 4:10). The Son was equally willing to share his inheritance, no matter what it might cost him. We know that adoptive parents go to great lengths to show no partiality to their own natural children, even though the natural fact of parenthood remains: they brought this one into the world, that other they adopted. Our adoption as children of God comes to us by courtesy of Jesus and the Father, it does not come to Jesus because of us and the Father.

Moods

The Holy Spirit, therefore, is seen or experienced as coming from God the First Person, down to us in Christ, then returning to God in the power of Christ. In other words, the Holy Spirit follows the same 'U' pattern I have often referred to. The 'doorway' pattern, which is the exact opposite of the way of the Spirit, leads to all sorts of confusion and darkness, one might say the shadow of the Holy Spirit, and is what happens when the way of the Spirit is flouted or neglected. There is always trouble if I try to reverse the process of the Spirit, going against the movement of the Spirit. Reversing the right process means putting my love for God before God's love for me.

Trouble comes when I try to earn God's love as a right, not just in gratitude. Trouble comes when I think that by keeping all the rules I will automatically walk into heaven. Trouble comes when I start looking down on those who do not keep the rules as well as I think I do. There is trouble when I despair or when I pretend, because I am unable to keep the rules. Trouble is there when I forget that God loves me for no 'reason' at all. The 'doorway' or 'shadow' way of proceeding is frequently found in the Old Testament because the way of the Old Testament was a learning process (compare Galatians 3:23–24) which we still mostly have to go through when young until we learn that love is unearned and unearnable.

There is a strong link between the Holy Spirit and whatever prevailing mood we find ourselves in, even our troubled moods. Once we can recognize our mood we can know what the Holy Spirit is saying to us at that time. If we take a broad spectrum of possible human moods, we may say our moods can vary from (0) away down in despair, close to suicide, to (1) deep clinical depression, to (2) depression where we can just begin to cope for ourselves, to (3) 'normal' depression, not needing medical supervision, to (4) slight depression, hardly noticeable, to (5) perfect balance, to (6) slight strain, to (7) growing tension, either of the 'panic' variety or the 'manic' variety, to (8) painful tension, to (9) unbalanced behaviour, to (10) breakdown, after which often comes despair or deep depression again. The deeper 'depression' moods feel like being in a yacht with no wind – and no engine – whereas the extremes of tension feel like being in a yacht in a hurricane. True peace is somewhere in the middle, like a yacht in a fine, strong breeze. The 'depression' moods feel like a guitar string not wound up at all, and giving no note, whereas the moods of over-strain feel like a guitar string ready to snap with being wound up too tightly. In that case a good healthy mood feels like a guitar string tuned to its proper note.[1]

To anyone in the depths of depression, the spirit that prevails in the 'doorway' mode is saying, 'You are worthless; you are rubbish. Your life is not worth living any more'. The Holy Spirit is saying, on the contrary, 'You are precious, you are God's child. You do not have to prove anything: just be there till I come to give you strength'. To one in a 'normal' strong depression, the 'doorway' mode suggests taking things easy, whereas the Spirit recognizes this as a time when we can lift ourselves out of the mood by coaxing ourselves to take an interest in life. To one in the centre of the moods, in perfect balance at what I called number (5) on the scale of moods, the only voice that is heard is the Holy Spirit, since this is where we truly belong. The deep feeling there is one of

gratitude and of peace and of being where God wants us
to be. To one under strain, whether slight or strong, the
Spirit is again reminding us we are God's children, and
that we will do better if we do not try to do everything
by ourselves. At the same time the shadow voice will be
telling us to try even harder, since we are really quite
wonderful. When we reach the outer limits of strain and
are in danger of breakdown, the 'doorway' mode will be
telling us, 'Final success is just around the corner. A last
effort should do it'. The Holy Spirit, on the other hand,
is reminding us strongly that God is the King, and the
responsibility does not all rest with the son or daughter.
'Stand down, and let others look after the situation.'

The perfect state of balance at number (5), on what
I call my 'Moodscale', coincides with recognizing my
status as God's child. I am God's child and therefore I
am not worthless – I am eternally precious. I am God's
child, not God, whereas in the very high numbers of the
scale I either behave as if I am God (when my mood
is manic) or behave as if all God's responsibility is on
my shoulders (when my mood is one of panic). Perfect
balance comes when the two truths are kept in balance:
I am from God, but I am not God. The First Person is
where I come from and where I go to. My origin is
precious, but a gift; and my final destiny is precious,
but a gift. The Holy Spirit is always guiding me to where
I call God 'Abba' (Romans 8:15), in the very centre of
my moods.

The First Person says, 'You are my child'. The Second
Person with and in me says 'Yes'. This is the movement
of the Spirit coming towards me, the dove whose eyes
I can see. The Second Person invites me in return to
love him in others, even where the love is rejected by
others. The First Person accepts that love as a token of
my gratitude. This is the movement of the Spirit leading
me forward, the dove whose eyes I cannot see. There are
two main times in which the Second Person asks me
to deny myself: when I feel lazy or reluctant, to show
gratitude and to make as big an effort as I can; when

I am straining and working too hard, to slow down and listen more carefully to the Spirit.

Once more may I return to the idea of the 'symphony' of the gospel in four movements? The first movement comes from the Father, adopting me as his child. In the second movement the Son in me accepts the adoption. In the third movement the Son invites me, along with him, to return the Father's love, and the very invitation inspires me to try. In the fourth movement the Father accepts that hopeful love as being of the same nature as his own love, and welcomes me home. My two pottery doves do not represent 'Father' and 'Son', but a two-way Relationship of love between them.

CHAPTER 16

FAITH BEFORE LOVE

'**F**aith is the beginning, and love is the end; and the union of the two together is God.' So says St Ignatius of Antioch, writing only seventy years after the death of Jesus.[1] Obviously, in one sense love comes first, when we mean that 'In this is love, not that we loved God but that he loved us . . .' (1 John 4:10). But from our own point of view as humans, faith is the beginning of everything, when we come to believe and trust in the love God has for us. Then, and only then, our love for God in return grows, as a reflection of God's love already shown to us, and as a gesture of gratitude to God. The first two movements of the symphony of the gospel have to do with God's gift and my faith, then the third and fourth movements have to do with God's call and my response of love.

The succession goes like this: Jesus says, 'As the Father has loved me, so have I loved you [my disciples]'; and 'I give you a new commandment, that you love one another. Just as I have loved you, you also should love one another' (John 15:9; 13:34 NRSV). The Father loves the Son, freely and with no conditions and without having been loved first. The Son comes into our world, trusts in the Father's love and reflects that kind of love upon each and every one of us, dying on the cross rather than leaving even the least of the little ones behind. Through the love Jesus mediated to us, we too come to trust in God's unbreakable, unshakable love, and Jesus gives us the new commandment, to love one another with that kind of love. He asks us to share with others the kind of love good parents have for their own children, and not just to share it with those who love us or belong to us, but to share it with all, even as far as the least of the little ones – even as far as those who hate us.

I am sure one could say with justification that according to Jesus himself the two greatest commandments of his own are, first, to trust in God's love for me, and secondly, to love all others in the way I have been loved by God, that is, in the way shown to me by Jesus. That is what this book has been all about. Preachers and teachers do not always seem to notice that when Jesus spoke about 'the two greatest commandments', he had been asked 'Teacher, which commandment *of the law* is the greatest?' (Matthew 22:36, NRSV; italics mine). His own 'one' commandment involves loving one another as he loved us, and that in turn means we have to have seen and believed in God's love shown to us through Jesus. How could we imitate, without having seen, and not just seen, but perceived? This, the love shown on the cross and accepted by God, is something that simply was not there in the Law, in the Old Covenant. The cross of Jesus, and his resurrection, was the dawn of the New Covenant, and of the new commandment.

In the letters of the same Ignatius of Antioch quoted at the start of this chapter, there are other sentences balancing faith and love. He links faith with the body of Christ, the bread, the humanity of Christ; he links love with the blood of Christ, with Christ's divinity, and with love as imperishable. 'Take a fresh grip on your faith (the very flesh of the Lord) and your love (the life-blood of Jesus Christ).'[2] 'I am fain for the bread of God, even the flesh of Jesus Christ, who is the seed of David; and for my drink I crave that blood of his which is love imperishable.'[3] 'Glory be to Jesus Christ, the Divine One who has filled you with such wisdom. I have seen how immovably settled in faith you are; nailed body and soul, as it were, to the cross of the Lord Jesus Christ, and rooted and grounded in love by his blood.'[4] Because we are human, we need faith; with faith, we become capable of being channels of divine love.

The tradition common to Matthew, Mark and Luke follows almost exactly the same order in each of the three Gospels, and it places faith before love, from the human point of view. Jesus trusts in the vision he receives at his baptism, and shares the Good News with us as his brothers and sisters. His effort is all directed to finding faith among his followers. They hear and hear, but do not understand; they see and see, but do not perceive. Then Peter sees and understands. Faith is seen as a pure gift, which comes even to those who do not ask for it since they do not know what it is; but faith may be prayed for on behalf of others, and shared by those who already have it. It could be said, anyone who prays for faith already has it. Love, on the other hand, needs also to be prayed for, personally, by those who do not have it, that is all of us. Even Jesus had to pray for the strength to stay faithful under murderous persecution. Even Peter, though he had faith, was not strong enough to show divine love by the fire in the courtyard, since he had not prayed for such love first. With faith Peter could be 'saved', but without first praying he could not show divine love. This second gift of the Spirit proceeds from the Son, who had to show it first, so we could know what we were asking for. Love is on the 'voluntary' side of the two-edged gospel, which means that we have to ask for it – the courteous God does not presume we will want it. We are all beggars not saviours, unless given divine love to love with.

Progress in Prayer

Faith grows into love, according to the Gospels. The seed of faith grows into a fruitful plant, which is itself a sower, dying to itself and thinking of the next generation. One of the key prayers at the start of the second half of the Synoptic Gospels is 'I believe; help my unbelief!' (Mark 9:24). This is the prayer Peter should have been praying,

but did not, at that time. He should also have prayed
as blind Bartimaeus did: 'My teacher, let me see again'
(Mark 10:51 NRSV). Peter had faith, and had seen Jesus
as the Christ, but he had gone blind again when it came
to believing in a Christ who suffers.

I wish now to trace the way through one of the classic
descriptions of progress in prayer and the spiritual life,
and to show how clearly it divides growth into faith
and love, in that order. My first acquaintance with
The Interior Castle, or, *The Mansions*, of St Teresa of
Avila, was many years ago, and I must confess to being
intrigued but mystified by it. I am very grateful to Ruth
Burrows' recent explanation,[5] which makes perfect sense
of a difficult text, and which has been a great comfort to
me and to many others. The central idea of Teresa's book
is to suggest that the reader compare him or herself to a
castle, in the heart of which is the throne of God. We start
our lives outside the castle, outside the moat; and our life
story is our search for God at the centre of ourselves. On
the way we move by stages from the outer rooms in to
the innermost rooms. She calls these stages 'mansions'
(stopping-off places), or 'suites of rooms' – there are seven
of them.

Teresa was not partial to Sisters in her communities
who were full of their wonderful experiences in prayer
but who were not to be found when there was hard work
to be done. On the other hand, she firmly believed that
those Sisters who were the backbone of the community
were also sure to be very well skilled in prayer, no matter
how little they might think of their own progress.

The first mansion has to do with me first being
attracted to God and starting to pray. The second
mansion I decide to take the search for God seriously,
whether alone or in company with others of like mind.
The third mansion is the stage where commitment is
suddenly or gradually seen to be not enough: I find I
cannot keep up the ideals, the devotions, the practices,
the sheer hard work for God I thought I would give
to him forever. I find I cannot keep my promises to

God. Teresa compared the first mansion to going a
long walk each day to the well with a bucket, the
second mansion to rigging up a complicated system of
pumps and pipes to bring the water to me, and the third
mansion to the time when the pumps and pipes break
down irretrievably.

Then comes a major barrier to be broken through, to
arrive at the fourth mansion. I have to come to the
realization that God loves me just as much, even though
I am weak, sinful, lazy, unable to keep my promises, and
generally helpless – it now becomes clearer that it makes
no real difference to the love God has for me. God loves
me though I am a sinner.

Once that truth has sunk in, I have understood the
Good News, as if for the first time, and I have faith,
as if for the first time. The wonderful truth I had not
dared to believe before, now becomes clear. I do not have
to earn heaven, because I could not. That should have
been obvious from the start, the knowledge that to reach
heaven is beyond me. So, having arrived in the fourth
mansion of the Good News, I am glad that I never quite
gave up praying, but that I clung to some minimal form
of prayer all along. I probably find the confidence now to
pray in whatever way suits me, regardless of the current
fashions in prayer. Little by little, like St Paul after his
conversion, I absorb the Good News into different areas
of my ordinary life.

The fifth mansion is a time of growth in confidence.
Life and prayer match one another better now. Knowing
the utter forgiveness of God, I can find my way around
the Bible more confidently, no longer feeling I am being
blasted with condemnation on every other page, knowing,
really, the difference between the way God seems when
my back is turned, and the way God really is when I
face squarely in his direction. I am also much more
ready to share the beauty of the gospel with others,
since I know it brings nothing but love to those who
face it.

The sixth mansion has to do with suffering. Not that

there was no suffering all along, but that once we have
passed through the first three mansions, suffering is
often harder to take. We remember Peter the apostle, and
his great joy at seeing who Jesus was, but then how hard
he found talk of suffering after that. A person is acutely
aware that God is love, so 'Why am I still suffering?'.
Sometimes it is the very confidence in preaching and
teaching the Good News that brings on persecution.
That was certainly the case with Jesus, and it is still
often true today. I myself have, at times, run into no
end of trouble for preaching the Good News so clearly.
Thus it comes about that prayer in the sixth mansion
may be very fragmented, but is wrung straight from
the heart.

There is, therefore, a barrier to be overcome before
reaching the seventh mansion: to believe that God loves
me even though I am suffering. This is really faith
grown into love. I learn to love God in gratitude for the
love originally shown to me and never withdrawn, even
though there is now apparently nothing in return.

Once the barrier is passed, the way to the seventh
mansion lies open. I would say the simplest way to
describe it is 'living in the present moment', which is
not Teresa's way of speaking but which fits: after the
first three mansions I am no longer worried about the
past; after the fourth, fifth and sixth mansions I am no
longer afraid of the future; all that is left is the present
moment, which is where God is for me.

For Teresa, contemplative prayer, or prayer where God
takes the initiative, starts with the fourth mansion. What
I have been calling the 'U' form of morality starts in
heaven, comes to me with unconditional love; then if
I believe and trust in that love, I make my return
of grateful service to God, but God's is the initiative,
since my motive is gratitude, not self-improvement. The
left-hand side of the two-edged gospel has to do with faith
and with the first three mansions spoken of by Teresa;
the right hand side has to do with spreading the Good
News and with continuing to love God when no felt love

is coming back, and concerns the fourth, fifth and sixth of the mansions. Anyone in the seventh mansion would be completely given over to God, and so completely fruitful. 'Faith is the beginning, love is the end; and the union of the two together is God.'

CHAPTER 17

NECESSARY; VOLUNTARY

B aptism has always been regarded as a sacrament necessary for salvation; confirmation, on the other hand, has more usually been regarded as optional. Of course, the baptism does not always and everywhere have to be a formal church ceremony with water being used and the right formula of words. In the usual church tradition, 'baptism of desire' has always been recognized as sufficient. What that comes to, is that the attitudes of mind belonging to the images on the left-hand side of my two-edged list are judged to be sufficient for salvation. If anyone, like the Good Thief, is willing to be forgiven for acts of malice and to have compassion shown to them for fundamental weakness, then that is enough. By comparison with such an attitude, colour, gender, age, creed, do not matter.

Confirmation, on the other hand, where celebrated by Christians, has been regarded as an optional sacrament. Sacraments do not celebrate human activities, but divine gifts. There can be no question of a confirmation candidate celebrating commitment, since commitment can and does break down. What does not break down is God's call, to the lamb to become a shepherd, to the child to become powerful, to the fish to become a fisher, and so on through the list. The call is always there, inviting even when our commitment breaks down.

Thus, baptism celebrates the gift of God, confirmation celebrates the call of God. The gift is offered to all: the recipient only needs to accept it, and then to respond, but not everyone responds by becoming a disciple. Salvation is necessary for a human being; discipleship is voluntary.

It will be obvious, too, that the 'symphony' of faith
growing into love is not played just once and never
again. Awareness of the gifts of God leads to generosity
in response to the gifts, which leads in its turn to a
greater understanding of them, and a further or greater
generosity, and so on.

How can Jesus' clear command, that we love one
another as he has loved us, ever be called 'voluntary'?
The response to the command is voluntary, in that it
is a response of gratitude, and it therefore depends
on our seeing first how much God has loved us. It is
also voluntary in that there is no absolute degree to
which it must be obeyed. We can never say, 'There,
I have obeyed Jesus' one command: I can sit back
now', nor can we say, 'I have failed miserably to obey
Jesus' one command: there is no point in trying any
more'. Forgiveness is always there, and I can always
try again, but without ever reaching the degree to which
Jesus loved me first. Matthew's version of the parable
of the king's son and the wedding feast always used
to puzzle me with the sting in its tail, where the man
with no wedding garment was given no mercy (Matthew
22:1–14). My puzzlement and disquiet disappeared on
the day someone suggested to me that by the custom
of the time, the wedding garment was provided by the
host, and so all the silent guest had to do was pick
one up and put it on. It does seem unlikely, in view
of Luke's version of the same story, that the poor and
maimed and blind and lame should be penalized for
not having a wedding garment they almost certainly
could not afford, when they had been pressed by the
king to come at short notice in the first place. Since
I began to look at Matthew's story in that light it has
seemed to me that the wedding garment, as far as I am
concerned, is God's forgiveness, and all I have to do is
pick it up and wear it. I do not have to pay for it; it is
quite beyond my power to provide it. All I can do is to
try and show by the quality of my life, that I appreciate
the gift.

Reflections from John's Gospel

I want to say a little at this stage about the 'I am'
statements of Jesus in John's gospel, and also about
John's manner of speaking of 'the disciple Jesus loved'.
'I am ... the light of the world, the way, the truth, the
life, the true vine, the good shepherd, the bread of life, the
gate of the sheepfold.' Also, '. . . before Abraham was, I
am' (John 8:58). Not quite the same, but in a similar vein,
Jesus says, 'I and the Father are one' (John 10:30). The
authority to apply the 'I am' titles to Christian disciples
is given in Matthew's Gospel, where in the Sermon on
the Mount Jesus says to his disciples, 'You are the light
of the world' (Matthew 5:14). Jesus sounds so majestic
in John's Gospel, when he proclaims that he is the Light
of the world. But then he shares the majestic title with
any and all of his disciples. If that 'I am' claim may be
shared with the disciples, why not the others? The First
Person of the Trinity is the first Light, Jesus is the true
reflection of the first Light, and the disciple is a true
reflection of Jesus. If a Christian founded on the rock of
Jesus may then become a rock for others, if a Christian
united with the divine wine may then become a channel
of that wine to others, why might not a Christian also
become the way for others, the truth for others, the life
for others, the true vine, the good shepherd, the bread of
life, and the gate of the sheepfold? Jesus himself is not
the first source of the Light, is not the first Rock, is not
the first origin of the true vine: the true Vine is the Love
that loves without having first been loved. Jesus is the
true reflection of such love.

An observation regarding 'the disciple Jesus loved':
the Jerusalem Bible translation of the prologue of John's
gospel ends like this: 'No one has ever seen God; it is
the only Son, who is nearest to the Father's heart, who
has made him known' (John 1:18). Now according to
the wording in the original Greek, that could mean 'the
disciple Jesus loved' was nearest to Jesus' heart at the
Last Supper (compare John 13:23), since the wording is

almost identical in both cases, and I would be certain
John meant it to be so. 'As the Father has loved me,
so have I loved you; *just as* I have loved you. you also
should love one another' (John 15:9; 13:34 NRSV; italics
mine). For myself, I am sure John wished his hearers and
readers to identify with 'the disciple Jesus loved' and to
see themselves as nearest to the heart of Jesus – Jesus
who like his Father has no favourites.

What about Jesus' saying, 'Before Abraham was, I
am'? Is there any way in which that is passed on by Jesus
to the one he saves and invites to become his disciple? I
think the answer is yes, since there is a sense in which
the least member of the kingdom is greater than John
the Baptist was, precisely for this reason. Any Christian
can say, 'Before Abraham was, I am God's adopted
child', because every Christian knows that he or she was
chosen in Christ before the foundation of the world (see
Ephesians 1:4–5). In some such secondary sense, also, I
would think any Christian may hope to say, 'In Christ, I
and the Father are one'. There is one true Light, and but
one true Reflection; but they have chosen to pass on to the
world of humanity their power of love-in-return-for-love,
so that 'As you, Father, are in me and I am in you, may
they also be one in us' (John 17:21 NRSV). As a Christian
I can say, 'I am not worthless, I am God's child', but also
'I am God's child, I am not God'. Sufferings come, we each
have a cross to carry, and it is often not in our own power
to end the sufferings. However, they enable us to love
God in the way Christ loved us, in imitation of the way
his Father loved him.

In summary, it is necessary for us to allow ourselves
to be adopted by God, but the extent to which we allow
God to work through us is voluntary. The love within the
Trinity is voluntary, and if ours is to reflect the love of
God, ours must be voluntary too.

CHAPTER 18

WATER; FIRE

The final contrast of biblical images I wish to apply to the notion of a 'two-edged gospel' is the contrast between water and fire. When the Spirit comes to us in baptism, the pervading image used within the ceremony is that of water. Water is used to forgive and to wash, to mark the candidate as being now a child of God, to mark the boundary between slavery in Egypt and freedom, between being outside the promised land and being across the Jordan within the kingdom; water speaks of the flood cleansing the whole earth and restoring life to the world and friendship between human beings and God. Water speaks of the power to destroy the whole legion of the demonic forces (see Mark 5:1–20).

Fire, on the other hand, belongs rather with the further coming of the Holy Spirit in our lives, the coming that belongs with the 'call' that follows baptism rather than with the pure 'gift' of baptism itself. The one grows out of the other: the gift is so great it inspires us to burst into flames of gratitude, as it were, and give generously to God in return. Such was the secret of the story of Zacchaeus, which we have mentioned more than once. Jesus was so generous with him, Zacchaeus erupted in a very generous response, giving half his enormous wealth to the poor, and so on.

Water belongs with the baptism of John which Jesus underwent. Fire, and strong light, belong with the transfiguration of Jesus. There is a candle of fire at our baptism, but it is for the comfort of the one being baptized. In our confirmation or transfiguration, the

light and fire are there to shine through the candidate
to others. The transformation of Peter from a boaster to
a humble instrument of God was effected at a fire: the
rock was refined and the pure gold emerged. The most
visible coming of the Spirit, at the first Pentecost after
Jesus' death and resurrection, was in the form of fire,
and not just fire but *tongues* of fire distributed among
those present (Acts 2:3). Tongues are for witnessing, for
speaking out God's goodness to all sinners, no matter
what the witnessing may cost. This second coming of the
Spirit, or rather this second direction in which the Spirit
faces within us, belongs with the right-hand side of my
list of the two-edged gospel.

There is a curious story in the First Book of Kings
which for all its strangeness seems to me to illustrate
beautifully the contrast between the water and the fire.
After the prophets of Baal had failed to pray their
sacrifice into flames, Elijah soaked his sacrifice with
twelve jars of water, prayed to God, and fire came down
and consumed sacrifice, altar, water and everything (see
1 Kings 18:20–40). So it is with us: God comes gently
and soothingly and the sheer surprise and delight of
such gentle coming kindles a flame of gratitude within
us which nothing can put out.

She and He

To conclude I wish to connect the whole thesis of this
book with the way Jesus refers to God as his Father
and our Father, and not just any father but the one
to be called 'Abba'. The key is there in the truth that
the First Person of the Trinity is the one who loved
and who loves without having been loved first by any
other person. The light of the First Person penetrates the
Second Person and makes the Second Person fruitful in
love. That way round, not the other way round. The light
of the Second Person returns to the First Person and is
recognized as being of the same divine nature. Moreover,
the light of the First Person penetrates me and makes me

fruitful. It is as simple as that, and as irreversible as that,
I believe.

Love-in-return-for-love cannot exist, cannot begin, without the initial Love coming from outside. By 'from
outside', I mean love that is not generated by the
loveliness of any other, but which is given for no reason.
A field can never produce a clean and useful crop without
the farmer to sow and tend it. The farmer cannot have
a crop without the field – that is also true. For the kind
of love there is in the Trinity, there must be one who
loves for no reason at all, and freely; one who accepts
the love freely and gives love freely in return of such a
kind that is freely accepted; and thirdly, there will be the
resulting relationship of mutual and freely-given love and
acceptance between them. Human married love and other
deep relationships of friendship are based on the love of
the Trinity, with the essential difference that human love
is always love given by one-who-has-already-been-loved,
loved by God if not by many others. The start of it all
is the First Person of the Trinity, who is called by Jesus
'Father', and not 'man-like'.

Even the Second Person of the Trinity would be like
a dark surface unless the Light shone. The light Jesus
shines upon us is reflected light, but is of the same
nature as the original Light: it is love against all reason.
Given that God the First Person is Father because he
is the one who comes from outside, penetrates and
makes fruitful what was before only able-to-be-fruitful,
the reason then why God is 'Abba' and not some distant
father-figure is that God loves *me* for no reason at all.
There are absolutely no expectations. Hopes, yes, but no
expectations. Such a Father I can live with. Such a Father
I can be affectionate towards.

There is another facet of Jesus calling God 'Abba' and
of Jesus being our model in this as in the whole of our
relationship with the First Person: if I can call God, the
First Person, 'Abba', then I am a first-generation child
of God, not a distant descendant. It means that each
and every one of us is impregnated by God directly, by

God's light alone. It means that Jesus as mediator is not
Father, but is the one who by his death tears down the
veil between us and God, exposing God to the human
being and the human being to God. Jesus is Son, never
Father; he is the Word, not the Speaker; he is the Way,
not the Journey's End.

I am still happily convinced by the arguments of
Joachim Jeremias that the central message of the New
Testament is contained in the way Jesus has of calling
God his 'Abba', and that Jesus was the first person in
history to call God 'Abba', and share the experience with
the rest of us.[1] Jesus was also careful to limit the title
'Abba' to one Person, not sharing it with himself or with
anyone else. We are to have only one Father, the one in
heaven (Matthew 23:9). If that should make a Catholic
priest feel uncomfortable, it should also make every
father of a family feel uncomfortable, since it applies
to everyone except the First Person of the Trinity, the
only one worthy of the name 'Father', since God the First
Person is the only one who loves without having first been
loved. All other fatherhood is called such by analogy, not
by right. The Christ is our one Master or Teacher, never
our Father (Matthew 23:10). 'The word that you hear is
not mine but the Father's who sent me' (John 14:24).

Whoever does the will of God, that is, whoever lets
God be 'Abba', is Jesus' mother, brother, sister – but
pointedly not his father (Matthew 12:50; Mark 3:35;
Luke 8:21). I will return very soon to the presence of
'mother' there in those quotations. In the kingdom we
may find a hundredfold of brothers and sisters, mothers
and children, but pointedly not a hundredfold of fathers
(Mark 10:29–30).

Add to this the very many places where Jesus tells us
to call God Father as he does himself. For Jesus there are
only two fathers: God and the devil, the One who sows the
good seed and the one who sows the weeds, the One who
forgives and the hard taskmaster, the Father of God-like
children and the father of lies (compare John 8:42–47). I
cannot help feeling that St Paul was going a little beyond

the vision of Jesus in calling himself the father (in Christ
Jesus, through the gospel) of the Christians at Corinth,
when Jesus himself was so careful not to call himself, or
anyone else but God, 'Abba'.[2] Other titles of God Jesus
does accept and pass on to his disciples, as we have noted.
God is Light, Jesus is Light of the world, his disciples are
to be light of the world. God is Shepherd, Jesus is Good
Shepherd, his disciples are to be shepherds. God is King,
Jesus is a king, his disciples will inherit the kingdom.
But whereas God is 'Abba', Jesus is Son and servant,
never father, and his disciples are called to be sons or
daughters, and servants, never fathers.

What is to be said about the way translators of
the Gospels sometimes make Jesus say 'my son', 'my
daughter', 'my children', to people he heals or gathers
to himself? It seems clear to me that there is always good
manuscript evidence for holding that Jesus simply said to
the paralytic, for example, 'Son, your sins are forgiven',
that is 'Son of God, God has forgiven your sins', not
my son at all (Mark 2:5). Or again, to the woman who
touched his cloak, 'Daughter, your faith has made you
well' (Mark 5:34, NRSV), that is, 'Daughter of God, your
faith that God is your own Father has made you better'.
Yet again, Jesus by the lakeside calls to the disciples in
the boat, 'Children, you have no fish, have you?' (John
21:5; see also 13:33, NRSV). God's children, not Christ's
children, unless here Jesus sees himself as being like a
mother.

Julian of Norwich saw the Second Person as Mother,[3]
and taking the hint from her I would suggest that
the Second Person is the source and foundation of all
relationships except that of 'Father'. Jesus was quite
ready to compare himself to a mother-hen longing to
gather her chicks under her wings (Luke 13:34). The
Second Person of the Trinity is both Mother, penetrated
by the One Light and become fruitful, and Son and
Daughter, the only-begotten who is the image of the
begetter. Like Wisdom (a comparison made by Paul and
several early Church writers) '. . . she is a reflection of

eternal light, a spotless mirror of the working of God, and an image of his goodness.'[4]

There is a rather neglected saying of Jesus about mothers: 'Whoever does the will of God is my brother, and sister, and mother' (Mark 3:35). I have suggested that 'doing the will of God' must include calling God 'Abba' as Jesus did. Which makes me brother of Christ or sister of Christ . . . but mother of Christ? If I can be mother (of Christ in others who do not yet know him) as well as being brother or sister (of Christ and of my fellow Christians), surely such a combination of relationships is not beyond the powers of the Second Person of the Trinity? There are at least two distinct features of any mirror. Like a mirror and along with all other mirrors I can be receptive of light; and like any receptive mirror I can be the means of creating light elsewhere in others.

I hope readers will realize that I am not trying to undermine the ordination of women. Anything I have said about there being only one Father would exclude from ordination men just as much as women, if there were any excluding to be done. In fighting for the retention of 'Abba' and 'Father' as the right and Christian way to address God, I am simply defending the irreversible truth that God's undeserved love, whose source is the First Person of the Trinity, penetrates us, we do not penetrate God. That has been my constant experience, and I cannot say otherwise.

APPENDIX

THE TWO-EDGED GOSPEL

lamb	shepherd
enlightened	light for others
child	power
son/daughter	servant
built on rock	rock for others
fish	fisher
coin	coin-seeker
sown with seed	sower (fruitful)
guided on the Way	guide
waited on by God	servant/slave
Mary	Martha
Jesus baptized by John	Jesus transfigured
baptism	confirmation
bread and water	wine
free	costly
forgiven	forgiving
'You are my beloved . . .'	'This is my beloved . . . listen to him/her'
Spirit loves	Spirit calls (invites)
faith the response	love the response
necessary	voluntary
water	fire

NOTES

Chapter 7
1. George E. Ganss, SJ, *The Spiritual Exercises of St Ignatius*. A translation and commentary. (St Louis, Missouri: Institute of Jesuit Sources, 1992) p 121 paras. 313–315. The paragraph numbers are standard in all modern translations.

Chapter 9
1. Gerald O'Mahony, *Praying St Mark's Gospel* (London: Geoffrey Chapman, 1990).
2. *Ibid.* p 135f. See the two sketch maps showing the difference between the journeys in the two halves of the Gospel.

Chapter 11
1. e.g. Irenaeus, *Against Heresies* V 2:3. Compare 2 Corinthians 5:1; 1 Corinthians 15:44; Mark 14:57–58 and John 2:19ff. Also *The Epistle of Barnabas* 16: 'for in the days before we believed in God, our hearts were a rotten, shaky abode, and a temple only too truly made by hands . . .'
2. Mixing of water with wine was 'not indeed, a native Palestinian custom, but a Greek practice which was observed in Palestine in Christ's time'. Joseph A. Jungmann, *The Mass of the Roman Rite* (London, 1961) p 333.
3. Justin, *1 Apologia* 32, 'For as man did not make the blood of the vine, but God . . .' And again Justin, *Trypho* 76, 'It was not man that engendered the blood of the grape, but God'. He compares wine to the 'stone not cut by human hands' in Daniel 2:45. Irenaeus also calls wine 'heavenly' in this context, *Against Heresies* V 1:3.
4. The offertory prayer quoted here was originally a Christmas prayer, and is still used as such, in an adapted form, for the collect of December 17th in the Roman Rite.
5. 'In me there is left no spark of desire for mundane things, but only a murmur of living water that whispers within me, "Come to the Father"'. Ignatius of Antioch, *Epistle to the Romans*, 7. This Ignatius was martyred in AD 107.

6. Irenaeus, *Against Heresies* V 1:3. The practice was also condemned by St Cyprian, *Letters* 63.

Chapter 14
1. See for example Plato, *Philebus* 28c:6ff.; 30c2–e2; Aristotle *Metaphysics* 1071b3–1076a4. Compare Romans 1:19–21.

Chapter 15
1. See Gerald O'Mahony, *Finding the Still Point: Making Use of Moods* (Guildford: Eagle, 1993) for a fuller treatment of this section.

Chapter 16
1. Ignatius of Antioch, *To the Ephesians* 14.
2. Ignatius, *To the Trallians* 8.
3. Ignatius, *To the Romans* 7.
4. Ignatius, *To the Smyrnaeans* 1. References to Ignatius of Antioch are taken from *Early Christian Writings: The Apostolic Fathers* translated by Maxwell Staniforth (Penguin Classics, 1968).
5. See Ruth Burrows, *Interior Castle Explored* (London: Sheed and Ward, 1989).

Chapter 18
1. Joachim Jeremias, *The Central Message of the New Testament*, (London: SCM Press Ltd., 1965) pp 9–30.
2. 1 Corinthians 4:14–15; Philemon 10. However, in 1 Thessalonians 2:7, Paul compares himself and fellow apostles to a mother.
3. Julian of Norwich, *Revelations of Divine Love*, translated by Clifton Wolters (Penguin Classics, 1984). See especially Chapters 58–60.
4. Wisdom 7:26; 1 Corinthians 1:24–30; Colossians 2:3. See also, for example, Justin, *Trypho* 61; Tertullian, *Against Praxeas* 5–7.

Printed in the United Kingdom
by Lightning Source UK Ltd.
106315UKS00001B/103-534

9 780852 446386